THE TABLETS OF EBLA

CONCORDANCE AND BIBLIOGRAPHY

THE TABLETS OF EBLA

CONCORDANCE AND BIBLIOGRAPHY

by

Scott G. Beld, William W. Hallo
and
Piotr Michalowski

WINONA LAKE, INDIANA
EISENBRAUNS

Library of Congress Cataloging in Publication Data

Beld, Scott G.
    The tablets of Ebla.

    Bibliography: p. 59.
    1. Ebla tablets—Concordances. 2. Ebla tablets—
Bibliography. I. Hallo, William W. II. Michalowski,
Piotr. III. Ebla tablets. IV. Title.
DS99.E25B44   1984   939′.4   84-5939
ISBN 0–931464–21–8

Contents

Preface

This book contains a list of Ebla tablets published prior to January 1, 1984. Only texts which are available in full are included here. There is no mention of partial transliterations which have been cited in many publications on Ebla. The bibliography contains all books and articles which contain editions, copies, or photographs of tablets from Tell Mardikh. In addition a judicious selection of publications concerning the texts and languages of Ebla is included. This is not a full bibliography of all that has been written on Ebla, much of which can best be forgotten. Because this is a bibliography dealing mainly with texts, many important items, particularly on the archaeology of the site, have not been included.

The project began with a preliminary list by W. W. Hallo which was revised and updated by Scott Beld. The bibliography was provided by Piotr Michalowski. The final editorial work was done jointly by Beld and Michalowski.

The concordance was organized with the help of the main computer facilities at the University of Michigan in Ann Arbor. The files will be updated as soon as new texts are published and new editions of the concordance will be issued in the future.

Abbreviations

AAAS	Annales Archéologiques Arabes Syriennes.
AdE	Annali di Ebla. Rome. (unpublished preprint)
AfO	Archiv für Orientforschung. Graz.
AION	Annali dell'Istituto Orientale di Napoli.
Allevam.	= Archi 1980b.
Archives	= Pettinato 1981b.
ARET	Archivi reali di Ebla. Rome.
BA	The Biblical Archeologist. Ann Arbor.
BSMS	Bulletin of the Society for Mesopotamian Studies. Toronto.
BZ	Biblische Zeitschrift. Freiburg.
CBQ	Catholic Biblical Quarterly. Washington.
Consid.	= Archi 1980a.
CRAI	Comptes rendus de l'Académie des Inscriptions et Belles-Lettres. Paris.
CRRAI	Compte rendu de la Rencontre Assyriologique Internationale.
Ebla	= Matthiae 1981.
JNES	Journal of Near Eastern Studies. Chicago.
JSS	Journal of Semitic Studies. Manchester.
MAIS	Missione archeologica Italiana in Siria. Rome.
MANE	Monographs on the Ancient Near East. Malibou.
MEE	Materiali Epigrafici di Ebla. Naples.
OA	Oriens Antiquus. Rome.
OLA	Orientalia Lovaniensia Analecta. Leuven.
OrNS	Orientalia. Nova Series. Rome
RA	Revue d'Assyriologie. Paris.
RBI	Rivista Biblica Italiana. Brescia.

RendPARA	Rendconditi della Pontificia Accademia Romana di Archeologia. Rome.
RlA	Reallexikon der Assyriologie. Berlin-Leipzig.
RSO	Rivista degli Studi Orientali. Rome.
SEb	Studi Eblaiti. Rome.
SMS	Syro-Mesopotamian Studies. Malibu.
UF	Ugarit-Forschungen. Münster.
VO	Vicino Oriente. Rome.
VT	Vetus Testamentum.
ZA	Zeitschrift für Assyriologie und vorderasiatische Archaologie. Berlin.

Ebla Texts: 1974 Season

TM. 74.G.	MEE 1	Editor	Date	Publication	Photo
120	21	Pettinato	1981b	Archives 43	--
126	27	Pettinato	1981b	Archives 59	--

TM. 75.G.	MEE 1	Editor	Date	Publication	Photo
217	41	Pettinato	1981b	Archives 161-2	--
273	90	Pettinato	1981b	Archives 115-8	--
309	106	Archi	1979b	SEb 1:111-2	Fig. 35
309	106	Pettinato	1981b	Archives 120	--
336	125	Pettinato	1976d	RSO 50: 3-8	--
336	125	Pettinato	1981b	Archives 136-142	--
427	158	Pettinato	1974/77	AfO 25:2-23	yes
427	158	Pettinato	1981b	Archives 150	--
522	190	Pettinato	1974/77	AfO 25:32	--
522	190	Pettinato	1981b	Archives 151f.	--
730	--	Archi	1980b	Allevam. 2	--
1219	658	Archi	1980a	Consid. 23-4 n. 19	Pl. VII
1233	672	Archi	1981c	SEb 4 145-54	Fig. 42
1234	673	Archi	1980a	Consid. 19	Pl. VIII 3
1261	700	Pettinato	1980a	MEE 2:1	Pl. I-II
1264	703	Pettinato	1980a	MEE 2:2	Pl. III-IV
1265	704	Pettinato	1980a	MEE 2:3	--
1266	705	Pettinato	1980a	MEE 2:4	Pl. V
1267	706	Archi	1980a	Consid. 21-3	Pl. VI
1268	707	Pettinato	1980a	MEE 2:5	Pl. VI
1271	710	Pettinato	1980a	MEE 2:6	Pl. VII-VIII
1272	711	Archi	1980d	SEb 2:30	Fig. 6
1272	711	Archi	1981f	BiAr. 44:150	--
1274	714	Pettinato	1980a	MEE 2:7	Pl. IX-X
1278	717	Pettinato	1980a	MEE 2:8	Pl. XI-XII
1280	719	Pettinato	1980a	MEE 2:9	Pl. XIII
1281	720	Archi	1980b	Allevam. 2	Pl. I 5-6
1282	721	Pettinato	1980a	MEE 2:10	Pl. XIII
1289	728	Pettinato	1980a	MEE 2:11	Pl. XIV
1292	731	Pettinato	1980a	MEE 2:12	Pl. XV-XVI
1293	732	Archi	1980a	Consid. 16-21	Pl. V
1293	732	Pettinato	1980a	MEE 2:13	Pl. XVII
1295	734	Pettinato	1980a	MEE 2:14	Pl. XVIII-XIX
1296	735	Pettinato	1980a	MEE 2:15	--
1299	738	Archi	1981c	SEb 4:137-8	Fig. 37
1299	738	Pettinato	1980a	MEE 2:16	--
1300	739	Pettinato	1980a	MEE 2:17	Pl. XX-XXI
1301	740	Pettinato	1982a	MEE 4:73	Pl. XXIII
1302	741	Pettinato	1982a	MEE 4:74	Pl. XXIII
1305	744	Pettinato	1980a	MEE 2:18	--

TM. 75.G.	MEE 1	Editor	Date	Publication	Photo
1312	751	Pettinato	1981d	MEE 3:1	Pl. I
1316	755	Pettinato	1981d	MEE 3:61	Pl. XXXIV
1321	759	Pettinato	1980a	MEE 2:19	Pl. XXII-XXIII
1321	759	Pettinato	1980e	BA 43:206-7	--
1323	761	Pettinato	1980a	MEE 2:20	Pl. XXIV-XXV
1325	763	Pettinato	1980a	MEE 2:21	Pl. XXVI-XXVII
1327	765	Pettinato	1980a	MEE 2:22	Pl. XXVIII-XXIX
1331	769	Pettinato	1980a	MEE 2:23	Pl. XXX
1332	770	Pettinato	1980a	MEE 2:24	Pl. XXX
1332	770	Archi	1980b	Allevam. 20	Pl. VIII 3-4
1333	771	Archi	1980b	Allevam. 20	Pl. VIII 1-2
1336	774	Pettinato	1980a	MEE 2:25	Pl. XXXI-XXXII
1338	776	Pettinato	1980a	MEE 2:26	Pl. XXXIII-XXXIV
1339	777	Pettinato	1980a	MEE 2:27	Pl. XXXV-XXXVI
1342	780	Pettinato	1980a	MEE 2:28	Pl. XXX
1343	781	Pettinato	1980a	MEE 2:29	Pl. XXXVII-XXXVIII
1345	783	Edzard	1981a	ARET 2:14	Pl. XIV-XV
1345	783	Pettinato	1980a	MEE 2:30	Pl. XXXIX-XL
1346	784	Pettinato	1980a	MEE 2:31	--
1347	785	Pettinato	1980a	MEE 2:32	Pl. XLI-XLII
1349	787	Pettinato	1980a	MEE 2:33	Pl. XLIII-XLIV
1350	788	Pettinato	1980a	MEE 2:34	Pl. XLV
1353	791	Milano	1980	SEb 3:12-15	Fig. 2
1353	791	Alberti	1981	OA 20:38-43	--
1354	792	Pettinato	1980a	MEE 2:35	Pl. XLVI-XLVII

4

TM. 75.G.	MEE 1	Editor	Date	Publication	Photo
1357	795	Pettinato	1981b	Archives 190-194	--
1357	795	Pettinato	1980a	MEE 2:36	Pl. XLVIII-XLIX
1358	796	Pettinato	1980a	MEE 2:37	Pl. L-LI
1359	797	Pettinato	1980a	MEE 2:38	Pl. LII
1359	797	Pettinato	1981b	Archives 123-4	--
1360	798	Pettinato	1980a	MEE 2:39	Pl. LIII-LIV
1362	800	Pettinato	1980a	MEE 2:40	Pl. LV-LVI
1365	803	Pettinato	1980a	MEE 2:41	Pl. LVII-LVIII
1366	804	Pettinato	1980a	MEE 2:42	Pl. LIX
1368	806	Pettinato	1980a	MEE 2:43	Pl. LX-LXI
1370	808	Pettinato	1980a	MEE 2:44	Pl. LXII
1371	809	Pettinato	1980a	MEE 2:45	Pl. LXIII
1372	810	Pettinato	1980a	MEE 2:46	Pl. LXIII
1373	811	Pettinato	1980a	MEE 2:47	Pl. LXIV
1376	814	Pettinato	1980a	MEE 2:48	Pl. LXV-LXVI
1377	815	Pettinato	1979f	OLA 5:188-93	Pl. I-II
1377	815	Pettinato	1981b	Archives 169-172	--
1377	815	Pettinato	1980a	MEE 2:49	Pl. LXVII-LXVIII
1378	816	Pettinato	1980a	MEE 2:50	Pl. LXIX-LXX
1385	823	Pettinato	1981d	MEE 3:51	Pl. XXVI
1392	830	Pettinato	1981d	MEE 3:74	--
1394	832	Edzard	1981a	ARET 2:33	Pl. XXIX
1396	834	Pettinato	1981d	MEE 3:26	Pl. VIII
1398	836	Pettinato	1981d	MEE 3:2	Pl. II-III
1400	838	Pettinato	1981d	MEE 3:62	Pl. XXXV
1402	840	Milano	1980	SEb 3:2-4	Fig. 1
1404	842	Pettinato	1982a	MEE 4:75	Pl. XXIV
1415	853	Matthiae	1981	Ebla	Pl. between pp. 112 and 113
1415	853	Pettinato	1978b	OA 17:166-168	Pl. XIV-XV
1415	853	Pettinato	1981d	MEE 3:39	Pl. IX-X
1426	864	Pettinato	1982a	MEE 4:40	Pl. XIX-XX

TM. 75.G.	MEE 1	Editor	Date	Publication	Photo
1430	868	Pettinato	1981d	MEE 3:65	Pl. XXXVI
1430	868	Fronzaroli	1980c	SEb 3:65-6	Fig. 16
1444	882	Edzard	1981b	SEb 4:36-46	Fig. 14
1445	883	Pettinato	1982a	MEE 4:76	Pl. XXV
1447	885	Archi	1980a	Consid. 19 n. 29	Pl. VIII 1-2
1448	886	Pettinato	1982a	MEE 4:32	Pl. XVIII
1450	888	Pettinato	1981d	MEE 3:55	Pl. XXX
1451	889	Archi	1981a	SEb 4:6-8	Fig. 2
1452	890	Fronzaroli	1980	SEb 3:34-6	Fig. 9
1470	908	Archi	1981a	SEb 4:9	Fig. 4
1473	911	Edzard	1981a	ARET 2:19	Pl. XVII
1474	912	Edzard	1981a	ARET 2:20	Pl. XIX
1477	915	Pettinato	1981d	MEE 3:66	Pl. XXXVI
1480	918	Edzard	1981a	ARET 2:23	Pl. XX
1480	918	Pettinato	1981b	Archives 121	--
1488	926	Pettinato	1981d	MEE 3:6	Pl. IV
1488	926	Pettinato	1976a	OA 15:170	Pl. III
1500	938	Edzard	1981a	ARET 2:7	Pl. IX, XXXVI
1501	939	Pettinato	1979a	OA 18:339	Pl. XXXVI
1515	953	Archi	1980b	Allevam. 5	Pl. III 1-2
1519	957	Pettinato	1979a	OA 18:340	Pl. XXXVII
1521	959	Pettinato	1981d	MEE 3:44	Pl. XV-XVI
1527	965	Matthiae	1981	Ebla	Pl. between pp. 112 and 113
1541	979	Edzard	1981a	ARET 2:8	Pl. IX, XXXVII
1545	983	Edzard	1981a	ARET 2:24	Pl. XX
1547	985	Archi	1980b	Allevam. 4	Pl. II 1-2
1549	987	Edzard	1981a	ARET 2:25	Pl. XXI
1558	996	Archi	1980b	Allevam. 17-8	Pl. VI
1559	997	Matthiae	1981	Ebla	Pl. between pp. 112 and 113
1559	997	Archi	1981c	SEb 4:155-61	Fig. 43
1562	1000	Edzard	1981a	ARET 2:28	Pl. XXIII-XXIV
1564	1002	Archi	1981c	SEb 4:142-4	Fig. 39
1565	1003	Pettinato	1981d	MEE 3:67	Pl. XXXVII
1572	1010	Edzard	1981a	ARET 2:11	Pl. X
1574	1012	Archi	1980b	Allevam. 21-2	Pl. IX 1-2
1576	1014	Edzard	1981a	ARET 2:1	Pl. I
1582	1020	Archi	1980b	Allevam. 22	Pl. IX 3-4
1599	1037	Pettinato	1981b	Archives 168-9	--
1616	1054	Pettinato	1981d	MEE 3:63	Pl. XXXV
1619	1057	Pettinato	1979a	OA 18:340-1	Pl. XXXVII

TM. 75.G.	MEE 1	Editor	Date	Publication	Photo
1622	1060	Edzard	1981a	ARET 2:32	Pl. XXVIII
1624	1062	Edzard	1981a	ARET 2:26	Pl. XXII
1625	1063	Archi	1981a	SEb 4:10	Fig. 5
1627	1065	Pettinato	1979a	OA 18:342	Pl. XXXVIII
1628	1066	Edzard	1981a	ARET 2:21	Pl. XVIII
1629	1067	Pettinato	1977c	OA 16:258-9	Pl. XI
1630	1068	Pettinato	1981b	Archives 148-150	--
1630	1068	Pettinato	1977c	OA 16:260-2	Pl. XII
1631	1069	Edzard	1981a	ARET 2:31	Pl. XXVII
1636	1074	Pettinato	1981d	MEE 3:40	Pl. XI
1636	1074	Pettinato	1978b	OA 17:177	Pl. XVI
1637	1075	Edzard	1981a	ARET 2:27	Pl. XXII
1639	1077	Pettinato	1981d	MEE 3:68	Pl. XXXVII
1640	1078	Edzard	1981a	ARET 2:16	Pl. XVII
1644	1082	Edzard	1981a	ARET 2:2	Pl. II
1645	1083	Pettinato	1981d	MEE 3:69	Pl. XXXVIII
1646	1084	Edzard	1981a	ARET 2:3	Pl. III
1647	1085	Edzard	1981a	ARET 2:22	Pl. XX
1657	1095	Edzard	1981a	ARET 2:4	Pl. IV-V
1663	1101	Edzard	1981a	ARET 2:17	Pl. XVII, XXXVIII
1667	1105	Edzard	1981a	ARET 2:15	Pl. XVI
1669	1107	Archi	1980c	SEb 2:11-4	Fig. 4-5
1671	1109	Edzard	1981a	ARET 2:18	Pl. XVIII
1676	1114	Pettinato	1982a	MEE 4:77	Pl. XXVI
1677	1115	Pettinato	1981d	MEE 3:70	Pl. XXXVIII
1678	1116	Pettinato	1982a	MEE 4:78	Pl. XXVI
1682	1120	Pettinato	1980b	OA 19:62-3	Pl. III
1682	1120	Pettinato	1980e	BiAr 43:211	p. 210
1687	1125	Edzard	1981a	ARET 2:12	Pl. XI
1689	1127	Edzard	1981a	ARET 2:34	Pl. XXX
1692	1130	Pettinato	1981d	MEE 3:71	Pl. XXXIX
1693	1131	Pettinato	1981b	Archives 239-40	--
1693	1131	Pettinato	1981d	MEE 3:73	Pl. XL
1693	1131	Archi	1980f	SEb 3:63	Fig. 15
1700	1138	Archi	1982	AfO Beiheft 19: 179	Fig. 9-11
1721	1159	Archi	1980b	Allevam. 1	Pl. I 1-2
1722	1160	Pettinato	1979a	OA 18:342-3	Pl. XXXVIII
1724	1162	Archi	1980c	SEb 2:9-10	Fig. 2
1732	1170	Edzard	1981a	ARET 2:30	Pl. XXVI, XXXIX-XL
1734	1172	Pettinato	1982a	MEE 4:79	Pl. XXVII
1749	1187	Archi	1979a	SEb 1:91-3	Fig. 21-4

TM. 75.G.	MEE 1	Editor	Date	Publication	Photo
1753	1191	Edzard	1981a	ARET 2:29	Pl. XXV
1764	1202	Pettinato	1979c	OA 18:130-44	Pl. I-VI
1766	1204	Fonzaroli	1979a	SEb 1:4-5	Fig. 1-2
1767	1205	Archi	1980c	SEb 2:7-8	Fig. 1
1774	1212	Pettinato	1982a	MEE 4:24	Pl. XVII
1781	1219	Matthiae	1981	Ebla	Pl. between pp. 112 and 113
1782	1220	Edzard	1981a	ARET 2:5	Pl. VII-VIII
1812	1250	Archi	1980a	Consid. 19 n. 29	Pl. VIII 4
1816	1254	Pettinato	1979a	OA 18:343	Pl. XXXVIII
1822	1260	Pettinato	1981d	MEE 3:45	Pl. XVII-XVIII
1825	1263	Pettinato	1982a	MEE 4:47	Pl. XXI-XXII
1841	1279	Pettinato	1981b	Archives 167-8	--
1841	1279	Archi	1982	AfO Beiheft 19: 179-180	Fig. 4-5
1845	?	Archi	1980b	Allevam. 24-5	Pl. XI 3-4
1849	1287	Edzard	1981a	ARET 2:57	Pl. XXXIV
1856	1294	Edzard	1981a	ARET 2:35	Pl. XXVII
1858	1296	Archi	1980b	Allevam. 2	Pl. L 3-4
1859	1297	Edzard	1981a	ARET 2:42	Pl. XXXI
1866	1304	Archi	1981c	SEb 4:139-40	Fig. 41
1907	1345	Pettinato	1981d	MEE 3:52	Pl. XXVII
1908	1346	Archi	1982	AfO Beiheft 19: 179	Fig. 2-3
1912	1350	Pettinato	1981d	MEE 3:47	Pl. XX-XXI
1927	1365	Pettinato	1981d	MEE 3:48	Pl. XXII-XXIII
1947	1385	Pettinato	1981d	MEE 3:18	Pl. VI-VII
1951	1389	Pettinato	1976a	OA 15:172-6	--
1951	1389	Pettinato	1981d	MEE 3:7	Pl. V
1953	1391	Archi	1981c	SEb 4:132-4	Fig. 35
1964	1402	Archi	1981a	SEb 4:8-9	Fig. 3
1965	1403	Pettinato	1982a	MEE 4:80	--
1975	1413	Archi	1981a	SEb 4:2-3	Fig. 1
1987	1425	Archi	1981c	SEb 4:139	Fig. 38
2000	1438	Pettinato	1982a	MEE 4:4	Pl. I-X
2001	1439	Pettinato	1982a	MEE 4:10	Pl. XIII
2003	1441	Pettinato	1982a	MEE 4:11	Pl. XIV-XV
2004	1442	Pettinato	1982a	MEE 4:9	Pl. XII

TM. 75.G.	MEE 1	Editor	Date	Publication	Photo
2005	1443	Pettinato	1982a	MEE 4:5	Pl. XI
2006	1444	Pettinato	1982a	MEE 4:6	Pl. XI
2007	1445	Pettinato	1982a	MEE 4:8	Pl. XII
2008	1446	Pettinato	1982a	MEE 4:81	Pl. XXVIII-XXIX
2011	1449	Edzard	1981a	ARET 2:6	Pl. VI
2014	1452	Pettinato	1981d	MEE 3:59	Pl. XXXIII
2015	1453	Edzard	1981a	ARET 2:13	Pl. XII-XIII
2038	1476	Pettinato	1979a	OA 18:344-5	Pl. XXXIX
2048	1486	Archi	1982	AfO Beiheft 19:188	Fig. 24-25
2057	1495	Archi	1982	AfO Beiheft 19: 186-187	Fig. 20-21
2065	1503	Pettinato	1981b	Archives 165	--
2068	1506	Pettinato	1981b	Archives 165	--
2068	1506	Archi	1980c	SEb 2:7, n. 19	Fig. 3
2069	1507	Archi	1982	AfO Beiheft 19: 181	Fig. 7-8
2075	1513	Pettinato	1979c	OA 18:147-59	--
2096	1534	Pettinato	1977c	OA 16:263-70	--
2104	1542	Archi	1982	AfO Beiheft 19: 181	Fig. 6
2112	1550	Pettinato	1981b	Archives 163	--
2112	1550	Archi	1980b	Allevam. 24	Pl. XI 1-2
2115	1553	Matthiae	1981	Ebla	Pl. between pp. 112 and 113
2115	1553	--	1979	SEb 1	SEb 1 cover
2119	1557	Archi	1979c	SEb 1:48	Fig. 15
2122	1560	Archi	1980b	Allevam. 18	Pl. VII
2131	1569	Archi	1982	AfO Beiheft 19: 187-188	Fig. 22-23
2133	1571	Archi	1982	AfO Beiheft 19: 186	Fig. 18-19
2136	1574	Pettinato	1981b	Archives 106-7	--
2136	1574	Pettinato	1978a	Or. 47:51-2	Pl. VII
2146	1584	Edzard	1981a	ARET 2:10	Pl. X
2184	1622	Edzard	1981a	ARET 2:39	Pl. XXX
2185	1623	Edzard	1981a	ARET 2:58	Pl. XXXV
2189	1627	Edzard	1981a	ARET 2:40	Pl. XXXI
2193	1631	Edzard	1981a	ARET 2:27a	Pl. XXII
2195	1633	Pettinato	1979a	OA 18:346	Pl. XL
2196	1634	Pettinato	1980b	OA 19:62	Pl. IV
2196	1634	Pettinato	1980e	BiAr 43:211	p. 210
2198	1636	Pettinato	1981e	AION 41:142	Pl. I

TM. 75.G.	MEE 1	Editor	Date	Publication	Photo
2198	1636	Edzard	1980	SEb 3:121	Fig. 26
2198	1636	Pettinato	1981d	MEE 3:54	Pl. XXIX
2199	1637	Pettinato	1982a	MEE 4:82	Pl. XXX
2200	1638	Pettinato	1975/76	RendPARA 48:50-1	--
2200	1638	Pettinato	1981d	MEE 3:72	Pl. XXXIX
2200	1638	Pettinato	1981b	Archives 233	--
2201	1639	Pettinato	1982a	MEE 4:83	Pl. XXX
2202	1640	Pettinato	1982a	MEE 4:84	Pl. XXX
2204	1642	Edzard	1981a	ARET 2:38	Pl. XXX
2205	1643	Edzard	1981a	ARET 2:47	Pl. XXXIII
2206	1644	Edzard	1981a	ARET 2:52	Pl. XXXIV
2207	1645	Edzard	1981a	ARET 2:49	Pl. XXXV
2208	1646	Edzard	1981a	ARET 2:44	Pl. XXXII
2209	1647	Edzard	1981a	ARET 2:48	Pl. XXXIV
2210	1648	Edzard	1981a	ARET 2:50	Pl. XXXII
2211	1649	Edzard	1981a	ARET 2:41	Pl. XXXI
2212	1650	Edzard	1981a	ARET 2:56	Pl. XXXV
2214	1652	Edzard	1981a	ARET 2:53	Pl. XXXIV
2215	1653	Edzard	1981a	ARET 2:55	Pl. XXXV
2216	1654	Edzard	1981a	ARET 2:45	Pl. XXXI
2217	1655	Pettinato	1979a	OA 18:347	Pl. XL
2218	1656	Edzard	1981a	ARET 2:36	Pl. XXVII
2219	1657	Edzard	1981a	ARET 2:54	Pl. XXXV
2220	1658	Edzard	1981a	ARET 2:46	Pl. XXXIII
2222	1660	Archi	1980b	Allevam. 23	Pl. X
2224	1662	Archi	1982	AfO Beiheft 19:185-186	Fig. 14-16
2225	1663	Archi	1981c	SEb 4:140-1	Fig. 40
2228	1666	Edzard	1981a	ARET 2:37	Pl. XXX
2229	1667	Edzard	1981a	ARET 2:43	Pl. XXXII
2230	1668	Edzard	1981a	ARET 2:51	Pl. XXXIV
2231	1669	Pettinato	1981d	MEE 3:56	Pl. XXXI-XXXII
2231	1669	Pettinato	1978a	Or. 47:55-9	Pl. VII-XII
2238	1676	Pettinato	1979c	OA 18:161-75	Pl. VII-XII
2260	1698	Pettinato	1981d	MEE 3:53	Pl. XXVIII-XXIX
2265	1703	Edzard	1981a	ARET 2:9	Pl. IX
2284	1722	Pettinato	1982a	MEE 4:12	Pl. XVI
2300	1738	Pettinato	1982a	MEE 4:85	Pl. XXX
2306	1744	Archi	1980b	Allevam. 26-7	Pl. XII
2309	1747	Archi	1980b	Allevam. 6-9	Pl. IV 1-2
2310	1748	Biga	1981	SEb 4:25-6	Fig. 11
2313	1751	Biga	1981	Seb 4:29	Fig. 12

TM. 75.G.	MEE 1	Editor	Date	Publication	Photo
2316	1754	Biga	1981	SEb 4:30-1	Fig. 13
2318	1756	Pettinato	1982a	MEE 4:86	Pl. XXX
2349	1788	Archi	1980b	Allevam. 12-16	Pl. V
2354	1793	Pettinato	1982a	MEE 4:87	Pl. XXXI
2367	1806	Pettinato	1980c	OA 19:238-42	Pl. XIV-XV
2367	1806	Pettinato	1977a	Akk. 2:24-6	--
2367	1806	Edzard	1981c	SEb 4:89-97	--
2367	1806	Pettinato	1980c	OA 19:231-45	Pl. XIV-XV
2367	1806	Matthiae	1981	Ebla	Pl. between pp. 112 and 113
2377	1816	Archi	1979b	SEb 1:107-8	Fig. 33
2379	1818	Archi	1979b	SEb 1:107-8	Fig. 34
2384	1823	Pettinato	1981d	MEE 3:57	Pl. XXX
2395	1834	Pettinato	1982a	MEE 4:116	Pl. XXXII
2420	1859	Sollberger	1980	SEb 3:134-47	Fig. 27
2422	1861	Pettinato	1982a	MEE 4:115	--
2422	1861	Matthiae	1981	Ebla	Pl. between pp. 112 and 113
2429	1868	Matthiae	1981	Ebla	Pl. between pp. 112 and 113
2459	1898	Pettinato	1979a	OA 18:347-51	Pl. XLI-XLII
2500	1939	Pettinato	1980b	OA 19:62-3	Pl. IV
2500	1939	Pettinato	1980e	BiAr 43:211	p. 210
2515	1954	Pettinato	1981d	MEE 3:50	Pl. XXIV XXV
2540	1979	Pettinato	1982a	MEE 4:88	Pl. XXXI
2557	1996	Pettinato	1981d	MEE 3:46	Pl. XIX
2592	2031	Archi	1981c	SEb 4:135-6	Fig. 36
2627	2066	Archi	1982	AfO Beiheft 19:182-4	Fig. 12-13
2659	2095	Archi	1981d	SEb 4:181-9	Fig. 44
2661	2097	Archi	1981d	SEb 4:181-9	Fig. 44
2662	2098	Archi	1981d	SEb 4:181-9	Fig. 44
2663	2099	Archi	1981d	SEb 4:181-9	Fig. 44
3000	2100	Archi and Biga	1982	ARET 3:1	--
3001	2101	Archi and Biga	1982	ARET 3:2	Pl. I
3002	--	Archi and Biga	1982	ARET 3:3	--
3003	2102	Archi and Biga	1982	ARET 3:2	Pl. I

TM. 75.G.	MEE 1	Editor	Date	Publication	Photo
3004	2103	Archi and Biga	1982	ARET 3:4	--
3005	2104	Archi and Biga	1982	ARET 3:5	--
3006	2105	Archi and Biga	1982	ARET 3:3	--
3007	2106	Archi and Biga	1982	ARET 3:4	--
3008	2107	Archi and Biga	1982	ARET 3:6	--
3009	2108	Archi and Biga	1982	ARET 3:7	Pl. III
3010	2109	Archi and Biga	1982	ARET 3:8	--
3011	2110	Archi and Biga	1982	ARET 3:2	Pl. I
3012	2111	Archi and Biga	1982	ARET 3:7	Pl. III
3013	2112	Archi and Biga	1982	ARET 3:9	--
3014	2113	Archi and Biga	1982	ARET 3:10	--
3015	2114	Archi and Biga	1982	ARET 3:11	--
3016	2115	Archi and Biga	1982	ARET 3:12	--
3017	2116	Archi and Biga	1982	ARET 3:13	--
3018	2117	Archi and Biga	1982	ARET 3:14	--
3019	2118	Archi and Biga	1982	ARET 3:15	--
3020	2119	Archi and Biga	1982	ARET 3:16	--
3021	2120	Archi and Biga	1982	ARET 3:17	--
3022	2121	Archi and Biga	1982	ARET 3:18	--
3023	2122	Archi and Biga	1982	ARET 3:19	--
3024	2123	Archi and Biga	1982	ARET 3:20	--
3025	2124	Archi and Biga	1982	ARET 3:21	--
3026	2125	Archi and Biga	1982	ARET 3:22	--
3027	2126	Archi and Biga	1982	ARET 3:23	--

TM. 75.G.	MEE 1	Editor	Date	Publication	Photo
3028	2127	Archi and Biga	1982	ARET 3:24	--
3029	2128	Archi and Biga	1982	ARET 3:25	--
3030	2129	Archi and Biga	1982	ARET 3:26	--
3031	2130	Archi and Biga	1982	ARET 3:27	--
3032	2131	Archi and Biga	1982	ARET 3:28	--
3033	2132	Archi and Biga	1982	ARET 3:29	--
3034	2133	Archi and Biga	1982	ARET 3:30	--
3035	2134	Archi and Biga	1982	ARET 3:31	--
3036	2135	Archi and Biga	1982	ARET 3:32	--
3037	2136	Archi and Biga	1982	ARET 3:33	--
3038	2137	Archi and Biga	1982	ARET 3:34	--
3039	2138	Archi and Biga	1982	ARET 3:31	--
3041	2140	Archi and Biga	1982	ARET 3:35	Pl. II
3042	2141	Archi and Biga	1982	ARET 3:36	--
3045	2144	Archi and Biga	1982	ARET 3:37	--
3048	2147	Archi and Biga	1982	ARET 3:38	--
3049	2148	Archi and Biga	1982	ARET 3:39	--
3051	2150	Archi and Biga	1982	ARET 3:40	--
3052	2151	Archi and Biga	1982	ARET 3:41	--
3053	2152	Archi and Biga	1982	ARET 3:42	--
3054	2153	Archi and Biga	1982	ARET 3:43	--
3055	2154	Archi and Biga	1982	ARET 3:44	--
3056	2155	Archi and Biga	1982	ARET 3:44	--
3057	2156	Archi and Biga	1982	ARET 3:45	--

TM. 75.G.	MEE 1	Editor	Date	Publication	Photo
3058	2157	Archi and Biga	1982	ARET 3:46	--
3059	2158	Archi and Biga	1982	ARET 3:47	--
3060	2159	Archi and Biga	1982	ARET 3:48	--
3061	2160	Archi and Biga	1982	ARET 3:49	--
3062	2161	Archi and Biga	1982	ARET 3:50	--
3063	2162	Archi and Biga	1982	ARET 3:51	--
3064	2163	Archi and Biga	1982	ARET 3:52	--
3065	2164	Archi and Biga	1982	ARET 3:53	--
3066	2165	Archi and Biga	1982	ARET 3:54	--
3067	2166	Archi and Biga	1982	ARET 3:55	--
3068	2167	Archi and Biga	1982	ARET 3:56	--
3069	2168	Archi and Biga	1982	ARET 3:57	--
3070	2169	Archi and Biga	1982	ARET 3:58	--
3071	2170	Archi and Biga	1982	ARET 3:59	--
3072	2171	Archi and Biga	1982	ARET 3:60	--
3073	2172	Archi and Biga	1982	ARET 3:60	--
3074	2173	Archi and Biga	1982	ARET 3:61	--
3075	2174	Archi and Biga	1982	ARET 3:62	--
3076	2175	Archi and Biga	1982	ARET 3:63	--
3077	2176	Archi and Biga	1982	ARET 3:64	--
3078	2177	Archi and Biga	1982	ARET 3:65	--
3079	2178	Archi and Biga	1982	ARET 3:66	--
3080	2179	Archi and Biga	1982	ARET 3:67	--
3081	2180	Archi and Biga	1982	ARET 3:63	--

TM. 75.G.	MEE 1	Editor	Date	Publication	Photo
3082	2181	Archi and Biga	1982	ARET 3:68	--
3083	2182	Archi and Biga	1982	ARET 3:69	--
3084	2183	Archi and Biga	1982	ARET 3:70	--
3085	2184	Archi and Biga	1982	ARET 3:71	--
3086	2185	Archi and Biga	1982	ARET 3:72	--
3087	2186	Archi and Biga	1982	ARET 3:73	--
3088	2187	Archi and Biga	1982	ARET 3:74	--
3089	2188	Archi and Biga	1982	ARET 3:75	--
3090	2189	Archi and Biga	1982	ARET 3:76	--
3091	2190	Archi and Biga	1982	ARET 3:77	--
3092	2191	Archi and Biga	1982	ARET 3:78	--
3093	2192	Archi and Biga	1982	ARET 3:79	--
3094	2193	Archi and Biga	1982	ARET 3:80	--
3095	2194	Archi and Biga	1982	ARET 3:81	--
3096	2195	Archi and Biga	1982	ARET 3:82	--
3097	2196	Archi and Biga	1982	ARET 3:83	--
3098	2197	Archi and Biga	1982	ARET 3:84	--
3099	2198	Archi and Biga	1982	ARET 3:85	--
3100	2199	Archi and Biga	1982	ARET 3:86	--
3101	2200	Archi and Biga	1982	ARET 3:82	--
3102	2201	Archi and Biga	1982	ARET 3:87	--
3103	2202	Archi and Biga	1982	ARET 3:88	--
3104	2203	Archi and Biga	1982	ARET 3:89	--
3105	2204	Archi and Biga	1982	ARET 3:90	--

TM. 75.G.	MEE 1	Editor	Date	Publication	Photo
3106	2205	Archi and Biga	1982	ARET 3:91	--
3107	2206	Archi and Biga	1982	ARET 3:92	--
3108	2207	Archi and Biga	1982	ARET 3:93	--
3109	2208	Archi and Biga	1982	ARET 3:94	--
3110	2209	Archi and Biga	1982	ARET 3:95	--
3111	2210	Archi and Biga	1982	ARET 3:96	--
3112	2211	Archi and Biga	1982	ARET 3:97	--
3113	2212	Archi and Biga	1982	ARET 3:98	--
3114	2213	Archi and Biga	1982	ARET 3:99	--
3115	2214	Archi and Biga	1982	ARET 3:100	--
3116	2215	Archi and Biga	1982	ARET 3:100	--
3117	2216	Archi and Biga	1982	ARET 3:100	--
3118	2217	Archi and Biga	1982	ARET 3:101	--
3119	2218	Archi and Biga	1982	ARET 3:102	--
3121	2220	Archi and Biga	1982	ARET 3:103	--
3122	2221	Archi and Biga	1982	ARET 3:104	Pl. III
3123	2222	Archi and Biga	1982	ARET 3:105	--
3124	2223	Archi and Biga	1982	ARET 3:106	Pl. IV
3125	2224	Archi and Biga	1982	ARET 3:107	--
3126	2225	Archi and Biga	1982	ARET 3:108	--
3127	2226	Archi and Biga	1982	ARET 3:109	--
3128	2227	Archi and Biga	1982	ARET 3:110	--
3129	2228	Archi and Biga	1982	ARET 3:111	Pl. V
3131	2230	Pettinato	1982a	MEE 4:48	--
3132	2231	Archi and Biga	1982	ARET 3:112	--

TM. 75.G.	MEE 1	Editor	Date	Publication	Photo
3133	2232	Archi and Biga	1982	ARET 3:113	--
3134	2233	Archi and Biga	1982	ARET 3:114	--
3135	2234	Archi and Biga	1982	ARET 3:115	--
3136	2235	Archi and Biga	1982	ARET 3:116	--
3137	2236	Archi and Biga	1982	ARET 3:117	--
3138	2237	Archi and Biga	1982	ARET 3:118	--
3139	2238	Archi and Biga	1982	ARET 3:119	--
3140	2239	Archi and Biga	1982	ARET 3:120	--
3141	2240	Archi and Biga	1982	ARET 3:121	--
3142	2241	Archi and Biga	1982	ARET 3:122	--
3143	2242	Archi and Biga	1982	ARET 3:123	--
3144	2243	Archi and Biga	1982	ARET 3:124	--
3145	2244	Archi and Biga	1982	ARET 3:125	--
3146	2245	Archi and Biga	1982	ARET 3:126	--
3147	2246	Archi and Biga	1982	ARET 3:127	--
3148	2247	Archi and Biga	1982	ARET 3:128	--
3149	2248	Archi and Biga	1982	ARET 3:129	--
3150	2249	Archi and Biga	1982	ARET 3:130	--
3151	2250	Archi and Biga	1982	ARET 3:131	--
3152	2251	Archi and Biga	1982	ARET 3:132	--
3153	2252	Archi and Biga	1982	ARET 3:133	--
3154	2253	Archi and Biga	1982	ARET 3:134	--
3155	2254	Archi and Biga	1982	ARET 3:134	--
3156	2255	Archi and Biga	1982	ARET 3:135	--

TM. 75.G.	MEE 1	Editor	Date	Publication	Photo
3157	2256	Archi and Biga	1982	ARET 3:136	--
3158	2257	Archi and Biga	1982	ARET 3:134	--
3159	2258	Archi and Biga	1982	ARET 3:137	--
3160	2259	Archi and Biga	1982	ARET 3:138	--
3161	2260	Archi and Biga	1982	ARET 3:139	--
3162	2261	Pettinato	1982a	MEE 4:89	--
3163	2262	Pettinato	1982a	MEE 4:90	--
3164	2263	Archi and Biga	1982	ARET 3:140	--
3165	2264	Archi and Biga	1982	ARET 3:141	--
3166	2265	Archi and Biga	1982	ARET 3:142	--
3167	2266	Archi and Biga	1982	ARET 3:143	--
3168	2267	Archi and Biga	1982	ARET 3:144	--
3169	2268	Archi and Biga	1982	ARET 3:145	--
3170	2269	Archi and Biga	1982	ARET 3:146	--
3171	2270	Pettinato	1982a	MEE 4:57	--
3172	2271	Archi and Biga	1982	ARET 3:147	--
3173	2272	Archi and Biga	1982	ARET 3:148	--
3174	2273	Archi and Biga	1982	ARET 3:149	--
3176	2276b	Archi and Biga	1982	ARET 3:150	--
3177	2277	Archi and Biga	1982	ARET 3:151	--
3178	2278	Archi and Biga	1982	ARET 3:152	--
3179	2279	Archi and Biga	1982	ARET 3:153	--
3180	2280	Archi and Biga	1982	ARET 3:154	--
3181	2281	Archi and Biga	1982	ARET 3:155	--
3182	2282	Archi and Biga	1982	ARET 3:156	--
3183	2283	Archi and Biga	1982	ARET 3:157	--

TM. 75.G.	MEE 1	Editor	Date	Publication	Photo
3184	2284	Archi and Biga	1982	ARET 3:158	--
3185	2285	Archi and Biga	1982	ARET 3:159	--
3186	2286	Archi and Biga	1982	ARET 3:159	--
3187	2287	Archi and Biga	1982	ARET 3:160	--
3188	2288	Archi and Biga	1982	ARET 3:161	--
3189	2289	Archi and Biga	1982	ARET 3:162	--
3190	2290	Archi and Biga	1982	ARET 3:163	--
3191	2291	Archi and Biga	1982	ARET 3:164	--
3192	2292	Archi and Biga	1982	ARET 3:165	--
3193	2293	Archi and Biga	1982	ARET 3:166	--
3194	2294	Archi and Biga	1982	ARET 3:167	--
3195	2295	Archi and Biga	1982	ARET 3:168	--
3196	2296	Archi and Biga	1982	ARET 3:169	--
3197	2297	Archi and Biga	1982	ARET 3:170	--
3198	2298	Archi and Biga	1982	ARET 3:171	--
3199	2299	Archi and Biga	1982	ARET 3:172	Pl. IV
3200	2300	Archi and Biga	1982	ARET 3:173	Pl. V
3201	2301	Archi and Biga	1982	ARET 3:174	--
3202	2302	Archi and Biga	1982	ARET 3:175	--
3203	2303	Archi and Biga	1982	ARET 3:176	--
3204	2304	Archi and Biga	1982	ARET 3:177	--
3205	2305	Archi and Biga	1982	ARET 3:178	Pl. VI
3207	2307	Archi and Biga	1982	ARET 3:179	--
3208	2308	Archi and Biga	1982	ARET 3:180	--

TM. 75.G.	MEE 1	Editor	Date	Publication	Photo
3209	2309	Archi and Biga	1982	ARET 3:181	--
3210	2310	Archi and Biga	1982	ARET 3:182	--
3211	2311	Pettinato	1981d	MEE 3:12	--
3213	2313	Archi and Biga	1982	ARET 3:183	--
3214	2314	Archi and Biga	1982	ARET 3:184	--
3215	2315	Archi and Biga	1982	ARET 3:185	--
3216	2316	Archi and Biga	1982	ARET 3:186	--
3217	2317	Archi and Biga	1982	ARET 3:187	Pl. VIII
3218	2318	Archi and Biga	1982	ARET 3:178	Pl. VI
3219	2319	Archi and Biga	1982	ARET 3:188	--
3220	2320	Archi and Biga	1982	ARET 3:189	--
3221	2321	Archi and Biga	1982	ARET 3:190	--
3222	2322	Archi and Biga	1982	ARET 3:191	--
3223	2323	Archi and Biga	1982	ARET 3:192	Pl. VII
3224	2324	Archi and Biga	1982	ARET 3:193	--
3225	2325	Archi and Biga	1982	ARET 3:194	--
3226	2326	Archi and Biga	1982	ARET 3:194	--
3227	2327	Archi and Biga	1982	ARET 3:193	--
3228	2328	Archi and Biga	1982	ARET 3:195	--
3229	2329	Archi and Biga	1982	ARET 3:196	--
3230	2330	Archi and Biga	1982	ARET 3:197	--
3231	2331	Archi and Biga	1982	ARET 3:198	--
3232	2332	Archi and Biga	1982	ARET 3:199	--
3233	2333	Archi and Biga	1982	ARET 3:200	--
3234	2334	Archi and Biga	1982	ARET 3:201	--

TM. 75.G.	MEE 1	Editor	Date	Publication	Photo
3235	2335	Archi and Biga	1982	ARET 3:202	--
3236	2336	Archi and Biga	1982	ARET 3:203	--
3237	2337	Archi and Biga	1982	ARET 3:204	--
3238	2338	Archi and Biga	1982	ARET 3:205	--
3239	2339	Archi and Biga	1982	ARET 3:205	--
3240	2340	Archi and Biga	1982	ARET 3:206	--
3241	2341	Archi and Biga	1982	ARET 3:207	--
3242	2342	Archi and Biga	1982	ARET 3:200	--
3243	2343	Archi and Biga	1982	ARET 3:208	--
3244	2344	Archi and Biga	1982	ARET 3:209	--
3245	2345	Archi and Biga	1982	ARET 3:210	--
3246	2346	Archi and Biga	1982	ARET 3:211	--
3247	2347	Archi and Biga	1982	ARET 3:212	--
3248	2348	Archi and Biga	1982	ARET 3:213	--
3249	2349	Archi and Biga	1982	ARET 3:214	Pl. VIII
3250	2350	Archi and Biga	1982	ARET 3:215	--
3251	2351	Archi and Biga	1982	ARET 3:215	--
3252	2352	Archi and Biga	1982	ARET 3:216	--
3253	2353	Archi and Biga	1982	ARET 3:217	--
3254	2354	Archi and Biga	1982	ARET 3:218	Pl. VIII
3255	2355	Archi and Biga	1982	ARET 3:219	--
3256	2356	Archi and Biga	1982	ARET 3:220	--
3257	2357	Archi and Biga	1982	ARET 3:221	--
3258	2358	Archi and Biga	1982	ARET 3:222	--

21

TM. 75.G.	MEE 1	Editor	Date	Publication	Photo
3259	2359	Archi and Biga	1982	ARET 3:223	--
3260	2360	Archi and Biga	1982	ARET 3:224	--
3261	2361	Archi and Biga	1982	ARET 3:225	--
3262	2362	Archi and Biga	1982	ARET 3:226	--
3263	2363	Archi and Biga	1982	ARET 3:227	--
3264	2364	Archi and Biga	1982	ARET 3:228	--
3265	2365	Archi and Biga	1982	ARET 3:229	--
3266	2366	Archi and Biga	1982	ARET 3:230	--
3267	2367	Archi and Biga	1982	ARET 3:231	--
3268	2368	Archi and Biga	1982	ARET 3:232	--
3269	2369	Archi and Biga	1982	ARET 3:233	--
3270	2370	Archi and Biga	1982	ARET 3:234	--
3271	2371	Pettinato	1982a	MEE 4:39	--
3272	2372	Archi and Biga	1982	ARET 3:235	--
3273	2373	Archi and Biga	1982	ARET 3:236	Pl. VII
3274	2374	Archi and Biga	1982	ARET 3:237	--
3275	2375	Archi and Biga	1982	ARET 3:238	--
3276	2376	Archi and Biga	1982	ARET 3:239	--
3277	2377	Archi and Biga	1982	ARET 3:232	--
3278	2378	Archi and Biga	1982	ARET 3:240	--
3279	2379	Archi and Biga	1982	ARET 3:232	--
3281	2381	Archi and Biga	1982	ARET 3:241	--
3282	2382	Archi and Biga	1982	ARET 3:242	--
3283	2383	Archi and Biga	1982	ARET 3:243	--
3284	2384	Archi and Biga	1982	ARET 3:244	--

TM. 75.G.	MEE 1	Editor	Date	Publication	Photo
3285	2385	Archi and Biga	1982	ARET 3:245	--
3286	2386	Archi and Biga	1982	ARET 3:246	--
3287	2387	Archi and Biga	1982	ARET 3:247	--
3288	2388	Archi and Biga	1982	ARET 3:248	--
3289	2389	Archi and Biga	1982	ARET 3:244	--
3290	2390	Archi and Biga	1982	ARET 3:249	--
3291	2391	Archi and Biga	1982	ARET 3:250	--
3292	2392	Archi and Biga	1982	ARET 3:251	--
3293	2393	Archi and Biga	1982	ARET 3:214	Pl. VIII
3294	2394	Archi and Biga	1982	ARET 3:252	--
3295	2395	Archi and Biga	1982	ARET 3:253	Pl. X
3296	2396	Archi and Biga	1982	ARET 3:254	--
3297	2397	Archi and Biga	1982	ARET 3:255	--
3298	2398	Archi and Biga	1982	ARET 3:256	--
3299	2399	Archi and Biga	1982	ARET 3:257	--
3300	2400	Archi and Biga	1982	ARET 3:258	--
3301	2401	Archi and Biga	1982	ARET 3:259	--
3302	2402	Archi and Biga	1982	ARET 3:260	--
3303	2403	Archi and Biga	1982	ARET 3:261	Pl. IX
3304	2404	Archi and Biga	1982	ARET 3:262	--
3305	2405	Archi and Biga	1982	ARET 3:263	--
3306	2406	Archi and Biga	1982	ARET 3:264	--
3307	2407	Archi and Biga	1982	ARET 3:265	--
3308	2408	Archi and Biga	1982	ARET 3:266	--

TM. 75.G.	MEE 1	Editor	Date	Publication	Photo
3309	2409	Archi and Biga	1982	ARET 3:267	--
3310	2410	Archi and Biga	1982	ARET 3:268	--
3311	2411	Archi and Biga	1982	ARET 3:269	--
3312	2412	Archi and Biga	1982	ARET 3:270	--
3313	2413	Archi and Biga	1982	ARET 3:271	--
3314	2414	Archi and Biga	1982	ARET 3:272	--
3315	2415	Archi and Biga	1982	ARET 3:273	--
3316	2416	Archi and Biga	1982	ARET 3:274	--
3317	2417	Archi and Biga	1982	ARET 3:275	--
3318	2418	Archi and Biga	1982	ARET 3:276	--
3319	2419	Archi and Biga	1982	ARET 3:277	--
3320	2420	Archi and Biga	1982	ARET 3:278	--
3321	2421	Archi and Biga	1982	ARET 3:279	--
3322	2422	Archi and Biga	1982	ARET 3:280	--
3323	2423	Archi and Biga	1982	ARET 3:281	--
3324	2424	Archi and Biga	1982	ARET 3:282	--
3325	2425	Archi and Biga	1982	ARET 3:283	--
3326a	2426	Archi and Biga	1982	ARET 3:284	--
3326b+c	2426	Archi and Biga	1982	ARET 3:285	--
3327	2427	Archi and Biga	1982	ARET 3:286	--
3328	2428	Archi and Biga	1982	ARET 3:287	--
3329	2429	Archi and Biga	1982	ARET 3:288	--
3330	2430	Archi and Biga	1982	ARET 3:289	--
3331	2431	Archi and Biga	1982	ARET 3:290	--

TM. 75.G.	MEE 1	Editor	Date	Publication	Photo
3332	2432	Archi and Biga	1982	ARET 3:291	--
3333	2433	Archi and Biga	1982	ARET 3:292	--
3334	2434	Archi and Biga	1982	ARET 3:293	--
3335	2435	Archi and Biga	1982	ARET 3:294	--
3336	2436	Archi and Biga	1982	ARET 3:295	--
3337	2437	Archi and Biga	1982	ARET 3:296	--
3338	2438	Archi and Biga	1982	ARET 3:297	--
3339	2439	Archi and Biga	1982	ARET 3:298	--
3340	2440	Archi and Biga	1982	ARET 3:299	--
3341	2441	Archi and Biga	1982	ARET 3:300	--
3342	2442	Archi and Biga	1982	ARET 3:301	--
3343	2443	Archi and Biga	1982	ARET 3:302	--
3344	2444	Archi and Biga	1982	ARET 3:303	--
3345	2445	Archi and Biga	1982	ARET 3:304	--
3346	2446	Archi and Biga	1982	ARET 3:299	--
3347	2447	Archi and Biga	1982	ARET 3:305	--
3348	2448	Archi and Biga	1982	ARET 3:306	--
3349	2449	Archi and Biga	1982	ARET 3:307	--
3350	2450	Archi and Biga	1982	ARET 3:308	--
3351	2451	Archi and Biga	1982	ARET 3:309	--
3352	2452	Archi and Biga	1982	ARET 3:310	Pl. X
3353	2453	Archi and Biga	1982	ARET 3:311	--
3354	2454	Archi and Biga	1982	ARET 3:312	--
3355	2455	Archi and Biga	1982	ARET 3:313	--

TM. 75.G.	MEE 1	Editor	Date	Publication	Photo
3356	2456	Archi and Biga	1982	ARET 3:314	--
3357	2457	Archi and Biga	1982	ARET 3:315	--
3358	2458	Archi and Biga	1982	ARET 3:316	--
3359	2459	Archi and Biga	1982	ARET 3:317	--
3360	2460	Archi and Biga	1982	ARET 3:318	--
3361	2461	Archi and Biga	1982	ARET 3:319	--
3362	2462	Archi and Biga	1982	ARET 3:320	--
3363	2463	Archi and Biga	1982	ARET 3:321	--
3364	2464	Archi and Biga	1982	ARET 3:321	--
3365	2465	Archi and Biga	1982	ARET 3:320	--
3366	2466	Archi and Biga	1982	ARET 3:322	--
3367	2467	Archi and Biga	1982	ARET 3:322	--
3368	2468	Archi and Biga	1982	ARET 3:323	Pl. IX
3369	2469	Archi and Biga	1982	ARET 3:323	Pl. IX
3370	2470	Archi and Biga	1982	ARET 3:324	--
3371	2471	Archi and Biga	1982	ARET 3:325	--
3372	2472	Archi and Biga	1982	ARET 3:326	--
3373	2473	Archi and Biga	1982	ARET 3:327	--
3374	2474	Archi and Biga	1982	ARET 3:328	Pl. X
3375	2475	Archi and Biga	1982	ARET 3:329	--
3376	2476	Archi and Biga	1982	ARET 3:330	--
3377	2477	Archi and Biga	1982	ARET 3:331	--
3378	2478	Archi and Biga	1982	ARET 3:329	--
3379	2479	Archi and Biga	1982	ARET 3:332	--

TM. 75.G.	MEE 1	Editor	Date	Publication	Photo
3380	2480	Archi and Biga	1982	ARET 3:333	--
3381	2481	Archi and Biga	1982	ARET 3:334	--
3382	2482	Archi and Biga	1982	ARET 3:335	Pl. X
3383	2483	Archi and Biga	1982	ARET 3:336	Pl. XI
3384	2484	Archi and Biga	1982	ARET 3:337	--
3385	2485	Archi and Biga	1982	ARET 3:338	Pl. XI
3386	2486	Archi and Biga	1982	ARET 3:339	--
3387	2487	Archi and Biga	1982	ARET 3:340	--
3388	2488	Archi and Biga	1982	ARET 3:341	--
3389	2489	Archi and Biga	1982	ARET 3:342	Pl. XII
3390	2490	Archi and Biga	1982	ARET 3:343	--
3391	2491	Archi and Biga	1982	ARET 3:344	--
3392	2492	Archi and Biga	1982	ARET 3:345	--
3393	2493	Archi and Biga	1982	ARET 3:345	--
3394	2494	Archi and Biga	1982	ARET 3:345	--
3395	2495	Archi and Biga	1982	ARET 3:344	--
3396	2496	Archi and Biga	1982	ARET 3:346	--
3397	2497	Pettinato	1982a	MEE 4:92	--
3398	2498	Archi and Biga	1982	ARET 3:347	--
3399	2499	Archi and Biga	1982	ARET 3:348	--
3401	2501	Archi and Biga	1982	ARET 3:349	--
3402	2502	Archi and Biga	1982	ARET 3:350	--
3403	2503	Archi and Biga	1982	ARET 3:351	--
3404	2504	Archi and Biga	1982	ARET 3:352	--
3405	2505	Archi and Biga	1982	ARET 3:353	--

TM. 75.G.	MEE 1	Editor	Date	Publication	Photo
3406	2506	Archi and Biga	1982	ARET 3:354	--
3407	2507	Archi and Biga	1982	ARET 3:355	--
3408	2508	Pettinato	1982a	MEE 4:91	--
3410	2510	Archi and Biga	1982	ARET 3:356	--
3411	2511	Archi and Biga	1982	ARET 3:357	--
3412	2512	Pettinato	1982a	MEE 4:56	--
3413	2513	Archi and Biga	1982	ARET 3:358	--
3414	2514	Pettinato	1981d	MEE 3:13	--
3415	2515	Archi and Biga	1982	ARET 3:359	--
3416	2516	Archi and Biga	1982	ARET 3:360	--
3417	2517	Archi and Biga	1982	ARET 3:361	--
3418	2518	Archi and Biga	1982	ARET 3:362	--
3419	2519	Archi and Biga	1982	ARET 3:363	--
3420	2520	Archi and Biga	1982	ARET 3:364	--
3421	2521	Archi and Biga	1982	ARET 3:365	--
3422	2522	Archi and Biga	1982	ARET 3:366	--
3423	2523	Archi and Biga	1982	ARET 3:367	--
3424	2524	Archi and Biga	1982	ARET 3:368	--
3425	2525	Archi and Biga	1982	ARET 3:369	--
3426	2526	Archi and Biga	1982	ARET 3:370	--
3427	2527	Archi and Biga	1982	ARET 3:371	--
3428	2528	Archi and Biga	1982	ARET 3:372	--
3429	2529	Archi and Biga	1982	ARET 3:373	--
3432	2532	Pettinato	1982a	MEE 4:29	--
3433	2533	Pettinato	1982a	MEE 4:7	--
3434	2534	Pettinato	1982a	MEE 4:28	--
3435	2535	Archi and Biga	1982	ARET 3:374	--

TM. 75.G.	MEE 1	Editor	Date	Publication	Photo
3436	2536	Archi and Biga	1982	ARET 3:375	--
3437	2537	Archi and Biga	1982	ARET 3:376	--
3439	2539	Pettinato	1981d	MEE 3:43	Pl. XII-XIV
3439	2539	Archi and Biga	1982	ARET 3:377	Pl. XI
3439	2539	Archi	1981d	SEb 4:181-9	Fig. 44
3441	2541	Archi and Biga	1982	ARET 3:378	Pl. XIII
3443	2543	Archi and Biga	1982	ARET 3:379	--
3444	2544	Archi and Biga	1982	ARET 3:380	--
3445	2545	Archi and Biga	1982	ARET 3:381	--
3446	2546	Archi and Biga	1982	ARET 3:382	--
3447	2547	Archi and Biga	1982	ARET 3:383	--
3448	2548	Archi and Biga	1982	ARET 3:384	--
3449	2549	Archi and Biga	1982	ARET 3:385	--
3450	2550	Archi and Biga	1982	ARET 3:386	--
3451	2551	Archi and Biga	1982	ARET 3:387	--
3452	2552	Archi and Biga	1982	ARET 3:388	--
3453	2553	Archi and Biga	1982	ARET 3:389	--
3454	2554	Archi and Biga	1982	ARET 3:390	--
3455	2555	Archi and Biga	1982	ARET 3:391	--
3456	2556	Archi and Biga	1982	ARET 3:392	--
3457	2557	Archi and Biga	1982	ARET 3:393	--
3458	2558	Archi and Biga	1982	ARET 3:394	--
3459	2559	Archi and Biga	1982	ARET 3:395	--
3460	2560	Archi and Biga	1982	ARET 3:396	--
3461	2561	Archi and Biga	1982	ARET 3:397	--

TM. 75.G.	MEE 1	Editor	Date	Publication	Photo
3462	2562	Archi and Biga	1982	ARET 3:398	--
3463	2563	Archi and Biga	1982	ARET 3:399	--
3464	2564	Archi and Biga	1982	ARET 3:400	--
3465	2565	Archi and Biga	1982	ARET 3:401	--
3466	2566	Archi and Biga	1982	ARET 3:402	--
3467	2567	Archi and Biga	1982	ARET 3:403	--
3468	2568	Archi and Biga	1982	ARET 3:404	--
3469	2569	Archi and Biga	1982	ARET 3:405	--
3470	2570	Archi and Biga	1982	ARET 3:406	--
3471	2571	Archi and Biga	1982	ARET 3:407	--
3472	2572	Archi and Biga	1982	ARET 3:408	--
3473	2573	Archi and Biga	1982	ARET 3:409	--
3474	2574	Archi and Biga	1982	ARET 3:410	--
3475	2575	Archi and Biga	1982	ARET 3:411	--
3476	2576	Archi and Biga	1982	ARET 3:412	--
3477	2577	Archi and Biga	1982	ARET 3:413	--
3478	2578	Archi and Biga	1982	ARET 3:414	--
3479	2579	Archi and Biga	1982	ARET 3:415	--
3480	2580	Archi and Biga	1982	ARET 3:416	--
3481	2581	Archi and Biga	1982	ARET 3:417	Pl. XIII
3482	2582	Archi and Biga	1982	ARET 3:418	--
3483	2583	Archi and Biga	1982	ARET 3:419	Pl. XIII
3484	2584	Archi and Biga	1982	ARET 3:420	--
3485	2585	Archi and Biga	1982	ARET 3:421	--

TM. 75.G.	MEE 1	Editor	Date	Publication	Photo
3486	2586	Archi and Biga	1982	ARET 3:422	--
3487	2587	Archi and Biga	1982	ARET 3:423	--
3488	2588	Archi and Biga	1982	ARET 3:424	--
3489	2589	Archi and Biga	1982	ARET 3:425	--
3490	2590	Archi and Biga	1982	ARET 3:426	--
3491	2591	Archi and Biga	1982	ARET 3:427	--
3492	2592	Archi and Biga	1982	ARET 3:428	--
3493	2593	Archi and Biga	1982	ARET 3:429	--
3494	2594	Archi and Biga	1982	ARET 3:430	--
3495	2595	Archi and Biga	1982	ARET 3:431	--
3496	2596	Archi and Biga	1982	ARET 3:432	--
3497	2597	Archi and Biga	1982	ARET 3:433	--
3498	2598	Archi and Biga	1982	ARET 3:434	--
3499	2599	Archi and Biga	1982	ARET 3:435	--
3500	2600	Archi and Biga	1982	ARET 3:436	--
3501	2601	Archi and Biga	1982	ARET 3:437	--
3502	2602	Archi and Biga	1982	ARET 3:438	--
3503	2603	Archi and Biga	1982	ARET 3:439	--
3504	2604	Archi and Biga	1982	ARET 3:440	Pl. XIV
3505	2605	Archi and Biga	1982	ARET 3:441	--
3506	2606	Archi and Biga	1982	ARET 3:442	--
3507	2607	Archi and Biga	1982	ARET 3:443	--
3508	2608	Archi and Biga	1982	ARET 3:444	--
3509	2609	Archi and Biga	1982	ARET 3:445	Pl. XIII

TM. 75.G.	MEE 1	Editor	Date	Publication	Photo
3510	2610	Archi and Biga	1982	ARET 3:446	Pl. XIII
3511	2611	Archi and Biga	1982	ARET 3:447	--
3512	2612	Archi and Biga	1982	ARET 3:448	--
3513	2613	Archi and Biga	1982	ARET 3:449	--
3514	2614	Archi and Biga	1982	ARET 3:450	--
3515	2615	Archi and Biga	1982	ARET 3:451	--
3516	2616	Archi and Biga	1982	ARET 3:452	--
3517	2617	Archi and Biga	1982	ARET 3:453	--
3518	2618	Archi and Biga	1982	ARET 3:454	--
3519	2619	Archi and Biga	1982	ARET 3:455	--
3520	2620	Archi and Biga	1982	ARET 3:456	--
3521	2621	Archi and Biga	1982	ARET 3:457	--
3522	2622	Archi and Biga	1982	ARET 3:458	--
3523	2623	Archi and Biga	1982	ARET 3:459	--
3524	2624	Archi and Biga	1982	ARET 3:460	Pl. XV
3524bis	--	Archi and Biga	1982	ARET 3:461	--
3525	2625	Archi and Biga	1982	ARET 3:462	--
3526	2626	Archi and Biga	1982	ARET 3:463	Pl. XVI
3527	2627	Pettinato	1981d	MEE 3:3	--
3528	2628	Pettinato	1982a	MEE 4:1	--
3529	2629	Archi and Biga	1982	ARET 3:464	--
3530	2630	Archi and Biga	1982	ARET 3:465	--
3531	2631	Archi and Biga	1982	ARET 3:466	Pl. XVII-XVIII
3532	2632	Archi and Biga	1982	ARET 3:467	--
3533	2633	Archi and Biga	1982	ARET 3:468	--

TM. 75.G.	MEE 1	Editor	Date	Publication	Photo
3534	2634	Archi and Biga	1982	ARET 3:469	--
3535	2635	Archi and Biga	1982	ARET 3:470	--
3536	2636	Archi and Biga	1982	ARET 3:471	Pl. XIX
3537	2637	Archi and Biga	1982	ARET 3:472	--
3538	2638	Archi and Biga	1982	ARET 3:473	--
3539	2639	Archi and Biga	1982	ARET 3:474	--
3540	2640	Archi and Biga	1982	ARET 3:475	--
3541	2641	Archi and Biga	1982	ARET 3:476	--
3542	2642	Archi and Biga	1982	ARET 3:477	--
3543	2643	Archi and Biga	1982	ARET 3:478	--
3544	2644	Archi and Biga	1982	ARET 3:479	--
3545	2645	Archi and Biga	1982	ARET 3:480	--
3546	2646	Archi and Biga	1982	ARET 3:473	--
3547	2647	Archi and Biga	1982	ARET 3:481	--
3548	2648	Archi and Biga	1982	ARET 3:482	--
3549	2649	Archi and Biga	1982	ARET 3:483	--
3550	2650	Archi and Biga	1982	ARET 3:484	--
3551	2651	Archi and Biga	1982	ARET 3:485	--
3552	2652	Archi and Biga	1982	ARET 3:486	--
3553	2653	Archi and Biga	1982	ARET 3:487	--
3554	2654	Archi and Biga	1982	ARET 3:488	--
3555	2655	Archi and Biga	1982	ARET 3:489	--
3556	2656	Archi and Biga	1982	ARET 3:490	--
3557	2657	Archi and Biga	1982	ARET 3:491	--

33

TM. 75.G.	MEE 1	Editor	Date	Publication	Photo
3558	2658	Archi and Biga	1982	ARET 3:492	--
3559	2659	Archi and Biga	1982	ARET 3:493	--
3560	2660	Archi and Biga	1982	ARET 3:494	--
3561	2661	Archi and Biga	1982	ARET 3:495	--
3562	2662	Archi and Biga	1982	ARET 3:496	--
3563	2663	Archi and Biga	1982	ARET 3:497	--
3564	2664	Archi and Biga	1982	ARET 3:498	--
3565	2665	Archi and Biga	1982	ARET 3:499	--
3566	2666	Archi and Biga	1982	ARET 3:500	--
3567	2667	Archi and Biga	1982	ARET 3:501	--
3568	2668	Archi and Biga	1982	ARET 3:502	--
3569	2669	Archi and Biga	1982	ARET 3:503	--
3570	2670	Archi and Biga	1982	ARET 3:504	--
3571	2671	Archi and Biga	1982	ARET 3:505	--
3572	2672	Archi and Biga	1982	ARET 3:506	--
3573	2673	Archi and Biga	1982	ARET 3:507	--
3574	2674	Archi and Biga	1982	ARET 3:508	--
3575	2675	Archi and Biga	1982	ARET 3:509	--
3576	2676	Archi and Biga	1982	ARET 3:510	--
3577	2677	Archi and Biga	1982	ARET 3:511	--
3578	2678	Archi and Biga	1982	ARET 3:512	--
3579	2679	Archi and Biga	1982	ARET 3:513	--
3580	2680	Archi and Biga	1982	ARET 3:514	--
3581	2681	Archi and Biga	1982	ARET 3:515	--

TM. 75.G.	MEE 1	Editor	Date	Publication	Photo
3582	2682	Archi and Biga	1982	ARET 3:516	--
3583	2683	Archi and Biga	1982	ARET 3:517	--
3584	2684	Archi and Biga	1982	ARET 3:518	--
3585	2685	Archi and Biga	1982	ARET 3:519	--
3586	2686	Archi and Biga	1982	ARET 3:520	--
3587	2687	Archi and Biga	1982	ARET 3:521	Pl. XV
3588	2688	Archi and Biga	1982	ARET 3:522	--
3589	2689	Archi and Biga	1982	ARET 3:523	--
3590	2690	Archi and Biga	1982	ARET 3:524	--
3591	2691	Archi and Biga	1982	ARET 3:525	--
3592	2692	Archi and Biga	1982	ARET 3:526	--
3593	2693	Archi and Biga	1982	ARET 3:527	--
3594	2694	Archi and Biga	1982	ARET 3:528	--
3595	2695	Archi and Biga	1982	ARET 3:521	Pl. XV
3596	2696	Archi and Biga	1982	ARET 3:529	--
3597	2697	Archi and Biga	1982	ARET 3:530	--
3598	2698	Archi and Biga	1982	ARET 3:531	--
3599	2699	Archi and Biga	1982	ARET 3:532	--
3600	2700	Archi and Biga	1982	ARET 3:533	--
3601	2701	Archi and Biga	1982	ARET 3:534	--
3602	2702	Archi and Biga	1982	ARET 3:535	--
3603	2703	Archi and Biga	1982	ARET 3:536	--
3604	2704	Archi and Biga	1982	ARET 3:537	--
3605	2705	Archi and Biga	1982	ARET 3:538	--

TM. 75.G.	MEE 1	Editor	Date	Publication	Photo
3606	2706	Archi and Biga	1982	ARET 3:539	--
3607	2707	Archi and Biga	1982	ARET 3:540	--
3608	2708	Archi and Biga	1982	ARET 3:541	--
3609	2709	Archi and Biga	1982	ARET 3:541	--
3610	2710	Archi and Biga	1982	ARET 3:542	--
3611	2711	Archi and Biga	1982	ARET 3:543	--
3612	2712	Archi and Biga	1982	ARET 3:544	--
3613	2713	Archi and Biga	1982	ARET 3:545	--
3614	2714	Archi and Biga	1982	ARET 3:546	--
3615	2715	Archi and Biga	1982	ARET 3:547	--
3616	2716	Archi and Biga	1982	ARET 3:548	--
3617	2717	Archi and Biga	1982	ARET 3:549	--
3618	2718	Archi and Biga	1982	ARET 3:550	--
3619	2719	Archi and Biga	1982	ARET 3:551	--
3620	2720	Archi and Biga	1982	ARET 3:552	--
3621	2721	Archi and Biga	1982	ARET 3:553	--
3622	2722	Archi and Biga	1982	ARET 3:554	--
3623	2723	Archi and Biga	1982	ARET 3:555	--
3624	2724	Archi and Biga	1982	ARET 3:556	--
3625	2725	Archi and Biga	1982	ARET 3:557	--
3626	2726	Archi and Biga	1982	ARET 3:558	--
3627	2727	Archi and Biga	1982	ARET 3:559	--
3628	2728	Archi and Biga	1982	ARET 3:560	--
3629	2729	Archi and Biga	1982	ARET 3:561	--

TM. 75.G.	MEE 1	Editor	Date	Publication	Photo
3630	2730	Archi and Biga	1982	ARET 3:562	Pl. XVI
3631	2731	Archi and Biga	1982	ARET 3:563	--
3632	2732	Archi and Biga	1982	ARET 3:564	--
3633	2733	Archi and Biga	1982	ARET 3:565	--
3634	2734	Archi and Biga	1982	ARET 3:566	--
3635	2735	Pettinato	1982a	MEE 4:93	--
3636	2736	Archi and Biga	1982	ARET 3:567	--
3637	2737	Archi and Biga	1982	ARET 3:568	--
3638	2738	Archi and Biga	1982	ARET 3:569	--
3639	2739	Archi and Biga	1982	ARET 3:570	--
3640	2740	Archi and Biga	1982	ARET 3:571	--
3641	2741	Archi and Biga	1982	ARET 3:572	--
3642	2742	Archi and Biga	1982	ARET 3:573	--
3643	2743	Archi and Biga	1982	ARET 3:574	--
3644	2744	Archi and Biga	1982	ARET 3:575	--
3645	2745	Archi and Biga	1982	ARET 3:576	--
3646	2746	Archi and Biga	1982	ARET 3:577	--
3647	2747	Archi and Biga	1982	ARET 3:578	--
3648	2748	Archi and Biga	1982	ARET 3:579	--
3649	2749	Archi and Biga	1982	ARET 3:580	--
3650	2750	Archi and Biga	1982	ARET 3:581	--
3651	2751	Archi and Biga	1982	ARET 3:582	--
3652	2752	Archi and Biga	1982	ARET 3:583	--
3653	2753	Archi and Biga	1982	ARET 3:584	Pl. XX
3654	2754	Archi and Biga	1982	ARET 3:585	--

37

TM. 75.G.	MEE 1	Editor	Date	Publication	Photo
3655	2755	Archi and Biga	1982	ARET 3:586	Pl. XVII
3656	2756	Archi and Biga	1982	ARET 3:587	--
3657	2757	Archi and Biga	1982	ARET 3:588	--
3658	2758	Archi and Biga	1982	ARET 3:589	--
3659	2759	Archi and Biga	1982	ARET 3:590	--
3660	2760	Archi and Biga	1982	ARET 3:591	--
3661	2761	Archi and Biga	1982	ARET 3:592	--
3662	2762	Archi and Biga	1982	ARET 3:591	--
3663	2763	Archi and Biga	1982	ARET 3:593	--
3664	2764	Archi and Biga	1982	ARET 3:594	--
3665	2765	Archi and Biga	1982	ARET 3:595	--
3666	2766	Archi and Biga	1982	ARET 3:596	--
3667	2767	Archi and Biga	1982	ARET 3:597	--
3668	2768	Archi and Biga	1982	ARET 3:598	--
3669	2769	Archi and Biga	1982	ARET 3:599	--
3670	2770	Archi and Biga	1982	ARET 3:600	--
3671	2771	Archi and Biga	1982	ARET 3:601	--
3672	2772	Archi and Biga	1982	ARET 3:602	--
3673	2773	Archi and Biga	1982	ARET 3:603	--
3674	2774	Archi and Biga	1982	ARET 3:604	--
3675	2775	Archi and Biga	1982	ARET 3:605	--
3676	2776	Archi and Biga	1982	ARET 3:606	--
3677	2777	Archi and Biga	1982	ARET 3:607	--
3678	2778	Archi and Biga	1982	ARET 3:608	--

TM. 75.G.	MEE 1	Editor	Date	Publication	Photo
3679	2779	Archi and Biga	1982	ARET 3:609	--
3680	2780	Archi and Biga	1982	ARET 3:610	--
3681	2781	Archi and Biga	1982	ARET 3:611	--
3682	2782	Archi and Biga	1982	ARET 3:612	--
3683	2783	Archi and Biga	1982	ARET 3:613	--
3684	2784	Archi and Biga	1982	ARET 3:614	--
3685	2785	Archi and Biga	1982	ARET 3:615	--
3686	2786	Archi and Biga	1982	ARET 3:616	--
3687	2787	Archi and Biga	1982	ARET 3:617	--
3688	2788	Archi and Biga	1982	ARET 3:618	--
3689	2789	Archi and Biga	1982	ARET 3:619	--
3690	2790	Archi and Biga	1982	ARET 3:620	--
3691	2791	Archi and Biga	1982	ARET 3:621	--
3692	2792	Archi and Biga	1982	ARET 3:622	--
3693	2793	Archi and Biga	1982	ARET 3:623	--
3694	2794	Archi and Biga	1982	ARET 3:624	--
3695	2795	Archi and Biga	1982	ARET 3:625	--
3696	2796	Archi and Biga	1982	ARET 3:626	--
3697	2797	Archi and Biga	1982	ARET 3:627	--
3698	2798	Archi and Biga	1982	ARET 3:628	--
3699	2799	Archi and Biga	1982	ARET 3:629	--
3700	2800	Archi and Biga	1982	ARET 3:630	--
3701	2801	Archi and Biga	1982	ARET 3:631	--
3702	2802	Archi and Biga	1982	ARET 3:595	--

TM. 75.G.	MEE 1	Editor	Date	Publication	Photo
3703	2803	Archi and Biga	1982	ARET 3:632	--
3704	2804	Archi and Biga	1982	ARET 3:633	--
3705	2805	Archi and Biga	1982	ARET 3:634	--
3706	2806	Archi and Biga	1982	ARET 3:635	--
3707	2807	Archi and Biga	1982	ARET 3:636	--
3708	2808	Archi and Biga	1982	ARET 3:637	--
3709	2809	Archi and Biga	1982	ARET 3:638	--
3710	2810	Archi and Biga	1982	ARET 3:639	--
3711	2811	Archi and Biga	1982	ARET 3:640	--
3712	2812	Archi and Biga	1982	ARET 3:641	--
3713	2813	Archi and Biga	1982	ARET 3:642	--
3714	2814	Archi and Biga	1982	ARET 3:643	--
3715	2815	Archi and Biga	1982	ARET 3:644	--
3716	2816	Archi and Biga	1982	ARET 3:645	--
3717	2817	Archi and Biga	1982	ARET 3:646	--
3718	2818	Archi and Biga	1982	ARET 3:647	--
3719	2819	Archi and Biga	1982	ARET 3:648	--
3720	2820	Archi and Biga	1982	ARET 3:649	--
3721	2821	Archi and Biga	1982	ARET 3:650	--
3722	2822	Archi and Biga	1982	ARET 3:627	--
3723	2823	Archi and Biga	1982	ARET 3:651	--
3724	2824	Archi and Biga	1982	ARET 3:652	--
3725	2825	Archi and Biga	1982	ARET 3:653	--
3726	2826	Archi and Biga	1982	ARET 3:654	--

TM. 75.G.	MEE 1	Editor	Date	Publication	Photo
3727	2827	Archi and Biga	1982	ARET 3:655	--
3728	2828	Archi and Biga	1982	ARET 3:656	--
3729	2829	Archi and Biga	1982	ARET 3:657	--
3730	2830	Archi and Biga	1982	ARET 3:658	--
3731	2831	Archi and Biga	1982	ARET 3:659	--
3732	2832	Archi and Biga	1982	ARET 3:660	--
3733	2833	Archi and Biga	1982	ARET 3:661	--
3734	2834	Archi and Biga	1982	ARET 3:662	--
3735	2835	Archi and Biga	1982	ARET 3:662	--
3736	2836	Archi and Biga	1982	ARET 3:663	--
3737	2837	Archi and Biga	1982	ARET 3:664	--
3738	2838	Archi and Biga	1982	ARET 3:662	--
3739	2839	Archi and Biga	1982	ARET 3:665	Pl. XVII
3740	2840	Archi and Biga	1982	ARET 3:666	--
3741	2841	Archi and Biga	1982	ARET 3:667	--
3742	2842	Archi and Biga	1982	ARET 3:668	--
3743	2843	Archi and Biga	1982	ARET 3:669	--
3744	2844	Archi and Biga	1982	ARET 3:670	--
3745	2845	Archi and Biga	1982	ARET 3:671	--
3746	2846	Archi and Biga	1982	ARET 3:672	--
3747	2847	Archi and Biga	1982	ARET 3:673	--
3748	2848	Archi and Biga	1982	ARET 3:674	--
3749	2849	Archi and Biga	1982	ARET 3:675	--
3750	2850	Archi and Biga	1982	ARET 3:676	--

TM. 75.G.	MEE 1	Editor	Date	Publication	Photo
3751	--	Archi and Biga	1982	ARET 3:677	--
3752	--	Archi and Biga	1982	ARET 3:678	--
3753	--	Archi and Biga	1982	ARET 3:679	--
3754	--	Archi and Biga	1982	ARET 3:680	--
3755	--	Archi and Biga	1982	ARET 3:681	--
3756	--	Archi and Biga	1982	ARET 3:682	--
3757	--	Archi and Biga	1982	ARET 3:683	--
3758	--	Archi and Biga	1982	ARET 3:684	--
3759	--	Archi and Biga	1982	ARET 3:685	--
3760	--	Archi and Biga	1982	ARET 3:686	--
3761	--	Archi and Biga	1982	ARET 3:687	--
3762	--	Archi and Biga	1982	ARET 3:688	--
3764	--	Archi and Biga	1982	ARET 3:689	--
3765	--	Archi and Biga	1982	ARET 3:690	--
3766	--	Archi and Biga	1982	ARET 3:691	--
3768	--	Archi and Biga	1982	ARET 3:692	Pl. XXI
3769	--	Archi and Biga	1982	ARET 3:693	--
3770	--	Archi and Biga	1982	ARET 3:694	--
3771	--	Archi and Biga	1982	ARET 3:695	--
3772	--	Archi and Biga	1982	ARET 3:696	--
3773	--	Archi and Biga	1982	ARET 3:689	--
3774	--	Archi and Biga	1982	ARET 3:697	--
3775	--	Archi and Biga	1982	ARET 3:698	--
3776	--	Archi and Biga	1982	ARET 3:699	--

TM. 75.G.	MEE 1	Editor	Date	Publication	Photo
3777	--	Archi and Biga	1982	ARET 3:700	--
3778	--	Archi and Biga	1982	ARET 3:701	--
3779	--	Archi and Biga	1982	ARET 3:702	--
3780	--	Archi and Biga	1982	ARET 3:703	--
3781	--	Archi and Biga	1982	ARET 3:704	--
3782	--	Archi and Biga	1982	ARET 3:705	--
3783	--	Archi and Biga	1982	ARET 3:706	--
3784	--	Archi and Biga	1982	ARET 3:707	--
3785	--	Archi and Biga	1982	ARET 3:703	--
3786	--	Archi and Biga	1982	ARET 3:708	--
3787	--	Archi and Biga	1982	ARET 3:709	--
3788	--	Archi and Biga	1982	ARET 3:710	--
3789	--	Archi and Biga	1982	ARET 3:711	--
3790	--	Archi and Biga	1982	ARET 3:712	--
3791	--	Archi and Biga	1982	ARET 3:713	--
3792	--	Archi and Biga	1982	ARET 3:714	--
3793	--	Archi and Biga	1982	ARET 3:715	--
3795	--	Archi and Biga	1982	ARET 3:716	--
3796	--	Archi and Biga	1982	ARET 3:717	--
3797	--	Archi and Biga	1982	ARET 3:718	--
3798	--	Archi and Biga	1982	ARET 3:719	--
3799	--	Archi and Biga	1982	ARET 3:720	--
3800	--	Archi and Biga	1982	ARET 3:721	--
3801	--	Archi and Biga	1982	ARET 3:722	--

TM. 75.G.	MEE 1	Editor	Date	Publication	Photo
3802	--	Archi and Biga	1982	ARET 3:723	--
3803	--	Archi and Biga	1982	ARET 3:711	--
3804	--	Archi and Biga	1982	ARET 3:724	--
3805	--	Archi and Biga	1982	ARET 3:725	--
3806	--	Archi and Biga	1982	ARET 3:726	--
3807	--	Archi and Biga	1982	ARET 3:727	--
3808	--	Archi and Biga	1982	ARET 3:728	--
3809	--	Archi and Biga	1982	ARET 3:729	--
3810	--	Archi and Biga	1982	ARET 3:730	--
3811	--	Archi and Biga	1982	ARET 3:731	--
3812	--	Archi and Biga	1982	ARET 3:732	--
3813	--	Archi and Biga	1982	ARET 3:733	--
3814	--	Archi and Biga	1982	ARET 3:734	--
3815	--	Archi and Biga	1982	ARET 3:735	--
3816	--	Archi and Biga	1982	ARET 3:736	--
3817	--	Archi and Biga	1982	ARET 3:737	--
3818	--	Archi and Biga	1982	ARET 3:738	--
3819	--	Archi and Biga	1982	ARET 3:739	--
3820	--	Archi and Biga	1982	ARET 3:737	--
3821	--	Archi and Biga	1982	ARET 3:740	--
3822	--	Archi and Biga	1982	ARET 3:741	--
3823	--	Archi and Biga	1982	ARET 3:742	--
3824	--	Archi and Biga	1982	ARET 3:736	--
3825	--	Archi and Biga	1982	ARET 3:743	--

TM. 75.G.	MEE 1	Editor	Date	Publication	Photo
3826	--	Archi and Biga	1982	ARET 3:737	--
3827	--	Archi and Biga	1982	ARET 3:744	--
3828	--	Archi and Biga	1982	ARET 3:732	--
3829	--	Archi and Biga	1982	ARET 3:737	--
3830	--	Archi and Biga	1982	ARET 3:732	--
3831	--	Archi and Biga	1982	ARET 3:745	--
3832	--	Archi and Biga	1982	ARET 3:746	--
3833	--	Archi and Biga	1982	ARET 3:747	--
3834	--	Archi and Biga	1982	ARET 3:748	--
3835	--	Archi and Biga	1982	ARET 3:749	--
3836	--	Archi and Biga	1982	ARET 3:750	--
3837	--	Archi and Biga	1982	ARET 3:751	--
3838	--	Archi and Biga	1982	ARET 3:732	--
3839	--	Archi and Biga	1982	ARET 3:752	--
3840	--	Archi and Biga	1982	ARET 3:753	--
3841	--	Archi and Biga	1982	ARET 3:754	--
3842	--	Archi and Biga	1982	ARET 3:737	--
3843	--	Archi and Biga	1982	ARET 3:755	--
3844	--	Archi and Biga	1982	ARET 3:756	--
3845	--	Archi and Biga	1982	ARET 3:757	--
3846	--	Archi and Biga	1982	ARET 3:758	--
3847	--	Archi and Biga	1982	ARET 3:759	--
3848	--	Archi and Biga	1982	ARET 3:760	--
3849	--	Archi and Biga	1982	ARET 3:761	--

TM. 75.G.	MEE 1	Editor	Date	Publication	Photo
3850	--	Archi and Biga	1982	ARET 3:762	--
3851	--	Archi and Biga	1982	ARET 3:763	--
3852	--	Archi and Biga	1982	ARET 3:764	--
3853	--	Archi and Biga	1982	ARET 3:765	--
3854	--	Archi and Biga	1982	ARET 3:758	--
3855	--	Archi and Biga	1982	ARET 3:766	--
3856	--	Archi and Biga	1982	ARET 3:767	--
3857	--	Archi and Biga	1982	ARET 3:768	--
3858	--	Archi and Biga	1982	ARET 3:769	--
3859	--	Archi and Biga	1982	ARET 3:770	--
3860	--	Archi and Biga	1982	ARET 3:771	--
3861	--	Archi and Biga	1982	ARET 3:772	--
3862	--	Archi and Biga	1982	ARET 3:773	--
3863	--	Archi and Biga	1982	ARET 3:774	--
3864	--	Archi and Biga	1982	ARET 3:775	--
3865	--	Archi and Biga	1982	ARET 3:776	--
3866	--	Archi and Biga	1982	ARET 3:777	--
3867	--	Archi and Biga	1982	ARET 3:778	Pl. XX
3868	--	Archi and Biga	1982	ARET 3:779	--
3869	--	Archi and Biga	1982	ARET 3:780	--
3870	--	Archi and Biga	1982	ARET 3:781	--
3871	--	Archi and Biga	1982	ARET 3:782	--
3872	--	Archi and Biga	1982	ARET 3:783	--
3873	--	Archi and Biga	1982	ARET 3:784	--

TM. 75.G.	<u>MEE</u> 1	Editor	Date	Publication	Photo
3874	--	Archi and Biga	1982	<u>ARET</u> 3:785	--
3875	--	Archi and Biga	1982	<u>ARET</u> 3:786	--
3876	--	Archi and Biga	1982	<u>ARET</u> 3:776	--
3877	--	Archi and Biga	1982	<u>ARET</u> 3:787	--
3878	--	Archi and Biga	1982	<u>ARET</u> 3:788	--
3879	--	Archi and Biga	1982	<u>ARET</u> 3:775	--
3880	--	Archi and Biga	1982	<u>ARET</u> 3:789	--
3881	--	Archi and Biga	1982	<u>ARET</u> 3:790	--
3882	--	Archi and Biga	1982	<u>ARET</u> 3:791	--
3883	--	Archi and Biga	1982	<u>ARET</u> 3:792	--
3884	--	Archi and Biga	1982	<u>ARET</u> 3:788	--
3885	--	Archi and Biga	1982	<u>ARET</u> 3:793	--
3886	--	Archi and Biga	1982	<u>ARET</u> 3:794	--
3887	--	Archi and Biga	1982	<u>ARET</u> 3:795	Pl. XXII
3888	--	Archi and Biga	1982	<u>ARET</u> 3:796	--
3889	--	Archi and Biga	1982	<u>ARET</u> 3:797	--
3890	--	--	--	not assigned	--
3891	--	--	--	not assigned	--
3892	--	--	--	not assigned	--
3893	--	--	--	not assigned	--
3894	--	--	--	not assigned	--
3895	--	--	--	not assigned	--
3896	--	--	--	not assigned	--
3897	--	--	--	not assigned	--
3898	--	--	--	not assigned	--
3899	--	--	--	not assigned	--
3900	2851	Archi and Biga	1982	<u>ARET</u> 3:798	--
3901	2852	Archi and Biga	1982	<u>ARET</u> 3:799	--
3902	2853	Archi and Biga	1982	<u>ARET</u> 3:800	--

TM. 75.G.	MEE 1	Editor	Date	Publication	Photo
3903	2854	Archi and Biga	1982	ARET 3:801	--
3904	2855	Archi and Biga	1982	ARET 3:802	--
3905	2856	Archi and Biga	1982	ARET 3:803	--
3906	2857	Archi and Biga	1982	ARET 3:804	--
3907	2858	Archi and Biga	1982	ARET 3:805	--
3908	2859	Archi and Biga	1982	ARET 3:806	--
3909	2860	Archi and Biga	1982	ARET 3:807	--
3910	2861	Archi and Biga	1982	ARET 3:808	--
3911	2862	Archi and Biga	1982	ARET 3:809	--
3912	2863	Archi and Biga	1982	ARET 3:810	--
3913	2864	Archi and Biga	1982	ARET 3:811	--
3914	2865	Archi and Biga	1982	ARET 3:800	--
3915	2866	Archi and Biga	1982	ARET 3:812	--
3916	2867	Archi and Biga	1982	ARET 3:813	--
3917	2868	Archi and Biga	1982	ARET 3:814	--
3918	2869	Archi and Biga	1982	ARET 3:815	--
3919	2870	Archi and Biga	1982	ARET 3:816	--
3920	2871	Archi and Biga	1982	ARET 3:817	--
3921	2872	Archi and Biga	1982	ARET 3:818	--
3922	2873	Archi and Biga	1982	ARET 3:819	--
3923	2874	Archi and Biga	1982	ARET 3:820	--
3924	2875	Archi and Biga	1982	ARET 3:821	--
3925	2876	Archi and Biga	1982	ARET 3:822	--
3926	2877	Archi and Biga	1982	ARET 3:823	--

48

TM. 75.G.	MEE 1	Editor	Date	Publication	Photo
3927	2878	Archi and Biga	1982	ARET 3:824	--
3928	2879	Archi and Biga	1982	ARET 3:825	--
3929	2880	Archi and Biga	1982	ARET 3:826	--
3930	2881	Archi and Biga	1982	ARET 3:827	--
3931	2882	Archi and Biga	1982	ARET 3:828	--
3932	2883	Archi and Biga	1982	ARET 3:829	--
3933	2884	Archi and Biga	1982	ARET 3:830	--
3934	2885	Archi and Biga	1982	ARET 3:831	--
3935	2886	Archi and Biga	1982	ARET 3:832	--
3936	2887	Archi and Biga	1982	ARET 3:833	--
3937	2888	Archi and Biga	1982	ARET 3:834	--
3938	2889	Archi and Biga	1982	ARET 3:835	--
3939	2890	Archi and Biga	1982	ARET 3:836	--
3940	2891	Archi and Biga	1982	ARET 3:837	--
3941	2892	Archi and Biga	1982	ARET 3:838	--
3942	2893	Archi and Biga	1982	ARET 3:839	--
3943	2894	Archi and Biga	1982	ARET 3:840	--
3944	2895	Archi and Biga	1982	ARET 3:841	--
3945	2896	Archi and Biga	1982	ARET 3:842	--
3946	2897	Archi and Biga	1982	ARET 3:843	--
3947	2898	Archi and Biga	1982	ARET 3:844	--
3948	2899	Archi and Biga	1982	ARET 3:845	--
3949	2900	Archi and Biga	1982	ARET 3:846	--
3950	2901	Archi and Biga	1982	ARET 3:847	--

TM. 75.G.	MEE 1	Editor	Date	Publication	Photo
3951	2902	Archi and Biga	1982	ARET 3:848	--
3952	2903	Archi and Biga	1982	ARET 3:849	--
3953	2904	Archi and Biga	1982	ARET 3:850	--
3954	2905	Archi and Biga	1982	ARET 3:851	--
3955	2906	Archi and Biga	1982	ARET 3:852	--
3956	2907	Archi and Biga	1982	ARET 3:853	--
3957	2908	Archi and Biga	1982	ARET 3:854	--
3958	2909	Archi and Biga	1982	ARET 3:855	--
3959	2910	Archi and Biga	1982	ARET 3:856	--
3960	2911	Archi and Biga	1982	ARET 3:857	--
3961	2912	Archi and Biga	1982	ARET 3:858	Pl. XXII
3962	2913	Archi and Biga	1982	ARET 3:859	--
3963	2914	Archi and Biga	1982	ARET 3:860	Pl. XXIII
3964	2915	Archi and Biga	1982	ARET 3:860	Pl. XXIII
3965	2916	Archi and Biga	1982	ARET 3:861	--
3966	2917	Archi and Biga	1982	ARET 3:862	--
3967	2918	Archi and Biga	1982	ARET 3:863	--
3968	2919	Archi and Biga	1982	ARET 3:858	Pl. XXII
3969	2920	Archi and Biga	1982	ARET 3:855	--
3970	2921	Archi and Biga	1982	ARET 3:864	--
3971	2922	Archi and Biga	1982	ARET 3:865	--
3972	2923	Archi and Biga	1982	ARET 3:866	--
3973	2924	Archi and Biga	1982	ARET 3:867	--
3974	2925	Archi and Biga	1982	ARET 3:868	--

TM. 75.G.	MEE 1	Editor	Date	Publication	Photo
3975	2926	Archi and Biga	1982	ARET 3:869	--
3976	2927	Archi and Biga	1982	ARET 3:858	Pl. XXII
3977	2928	Archi and Biga	1982	ARET 3:870	--
3978	2929	Archi and Biga	1982	ARET 3:871	--
3979	2930	Archi and Biga	1982	ARET 3:872	--
3980	2931	Archi and Biga	1982	ARET 3:873	--
3981	2932	Archi and Biga	1982	ARET 3:874	--
3982	2933	Archi and Biga	1982	ARET 3:869	--
3983	2934	Archi and Biga	1982	ARET 3:875	--
3984	2935	Archi and Biga	1982	ARET 3:876	--
3985	2936	Archi and Biga	1982	ARET 3:877	--
3986	2937	Archi and Biga	1982	ARET 3:878	--
3987	2938	Archi and Biga	1982	ARET 3:879	--
3988	2939	Archi and Biga	1982	ARET 3:860	Pl. XXIII
3989	2940	Archi and Biga	1982	ARET 3:880	--
3990	2941	Archi and Biga	1982	ARET 3:881	--
3991	2942	Archi and Biga	1982	ARET 3:882	--
3992	2943	Archi and Biga	1982	ARET 3:883	--
3993	2944	Archi and Biga	1982	ARET 3:884	--
3994	2945	Archi and Biga	1982	ARET 3:885	--
3995	2946	Archi and Biga	1982	ARET 3:886	--
3996	2947	Archi and Biga	1982	ARET 3:887	--
3997	2948	Archi and Biga	1982	ARET 3:888	--
3998	2949	Archi and Biga	1982	ARET 3:889	--

TM. 75.G.	MEE 1	Editor	Date	Publication	Photo
3999	2950	Archi and Biga	1982	ARET 3:890	--
4000	2951	Archi and Biga	1982	ARET 3:882	--
4001	2952	Archi and Biga	1982	ARET 3:860	Pl. XXIII
4002	2953	Archi and Biga	1982	ARET 3:891	--
4003	2954	Archi and Biga	1982	ARET 3:892	--
4004	2955	Archi and Biga	1982	ARET 3:887	--
4005	2956	Archi and Biga	1982	ARET 3:881	--
4006	2957	Archi and Biga	1982	ARET 3:893	--
4007	2958	Archi and Biga	1982	ARET 3:894	--
4008	2959	Archi and Biga	1982	ARET 3:895	--
4009	2960	Archi and Biga	1982	ARET 3:885	--
4010	2961	Archi and Biga	1982	ARET 3:896	--
4011	2962	Archi and Biga	1982	ARET 3:887	--
4012	2963	Archi and Biga	1982	ARET 3:897	--
4013	2964	Archi and Biga	1982	ARET 3:898	--
4014	2965	Archi and Biga	1982	ARET 3:899	--
4015	2966	Archi and Biga	1982	ARET 3:900	Pl. XX
4016	2967	Archi and Biga	1982	ARET 3:901	--
4017	2968	Archi and Biga	1982	ARET 3:902	--
4018	2969	Archi and Biga	1982	ARET 3:903	--
4019	2970	Pettinato	1981d	MEE 3:19	--
4020	2971	Archi and Biga	1982	ARET 3:881	--
4021	2972	Archi and Biga	1982	ARET 3:904	--
4022	2973	Archi and Biga	1982	ARET 3:905	--
4023	2974	Archi and Biga	1982	ARET 3:860	Pl. XXIII

TM. 75.G.	MEE 1	Editor	Date	Publication	Photo
4024	2975	Archi and Biga	1982	ARET 3:906	--
4025	2976	Archi and Biga	1982	ARET 3:881	--
4026	2977	Archi and Biga	1982	ARET 3:907	--
4027	2978	Archi and Biga	1982	ARET 3:908	--
4028	2979	Archi and Biga	1982	ARET 3:909	--
4029	2980	Archi and Biga	1982	ARET 3:910	--
4030	2981	Archi and Biga	1982	ARET 3:911	--
4031	2982	Archi and Biga	1982	ARET 3:912	--
4032	2983	Archi and Biga	1982	ARET 3:913	--
4033	2984	Archi and Biga	1982	ARET 3:914	--
4034	2985	Archi and Biga	1982	ARET 3:915	--
4035	2986	Archi and Biga	1982	ARET 3:916	--
4036	2987	Archi and Biga	1982	ARET 3:917	--
4037	2988	Archi and Biga	1982	ARET 3:918	--
4038	2989	Archi and Biga	1982	ARET 3:919	--
4039	2990	Archi and Biga	1982	ARET 3:881	--
4040	2991	Archi and Biga	1982	ARET 3:920	--
4041	2992	Archi and Biga	1982	ARET 3:921	--
4042	2993	Archi and Biga	1982	ARET 3:922	--
4043	2994	Archi and Biga	1982	ARET 3:923	--
4044	2995	Archi and Biga	1982	ARET 3:924	--
4045	2996	Archi and Biga	1982	ARET 3:925	--
4046	2997	Archi and Biga	1982	ARET 3:861	--
4047	2998	Archi and Biga	1982	ARET 3:926	--

TM. 75.G.	MEE 1	Editor	Date	Publication	Photo
4048	2999	Archi and Biga	1982	ARET 3:927	--
4049	3000	Archi and Biga	1982	ARET 3:928	--
4050	3001	Archi and Biga	1982	ARET 3:929	--
4051	3002	Archi and Biga	1982	ARET 3:930	--
4052	3003	Archi and Biga	1982	ARET 3:931	--
4053	3004	Archi and Biga	1982	ARET 3:932	--
4054	3005	Archi and Biga	1982	ARET 3:933	--
4055	3006	Archi and Biga	1982	ARET 3:934	--
4056	3007	Archi and Biga	1982	ARET 3:935	--
4057	3008	Archi and Biga	1982	ARET 3:936	--
4058	3009	Archi and Biga	1982	ARET 3:937	--
4059	3010	Archi and Biga	1982	ARET 3:938	Pl. XXIV
4060	3011	Archi and Biga	1982	ARET 3:939	Pl. XXIV
4061	3012	Archi and Biga	1982	ARET 3:940	--
4062	3013	Archi and Biga	1982	ARET 3:941	--
4063	3014	Archi and Biga	1982	ARET 3:942	--
4064	3015	Archi and Biga	1982	ARET 3:943	--
4065	3016	Archi and Biga	1982	ARET 3:944	--
4066	3017	Archi and Biga	1982	ARET 3:945	--
4067	3018	Archi and Biga	1982	ARET 3:946	--
4068	3019	Archi and Biga	1982	ARET 3:947	--
4069	3020	Archi and Biga	1982	ARET 3:948	--
4070	3021	Archi and Biga	1982	ARET 3:949	--
4071	3022	Archi and Biga	1982	ARET 3:950	--

TM. 75.G.	MEE 1	Editor	Date	Publication	Photo
4072	3023	Archi and Biga	1982	ARET 3:951	--
4073	3024	Archi and Biga	1982	ARET 3:952	--
4074	3025	Archi and Biga	1982	ARET 3:953	--
4075	3026	Archi and Biga	1982	ARET 3:954	--
4076	3027	Archi and Biga	1982	ARET 3:955	--
4077	3028	Archi and Biga	1982	ARET 3:956	--
4078	3029	Archi and Biga	1982	ARET 3:957	--
4079	3030	Archi and Biga	1982	ARET 3:958	--
4080	3031	Archi and Biga	1982	ARET 3:959	--
4081	3032	Archi and Biga	1982	ARET 3:960	--
4082	3033	Archi and Biga	1982	ARET 3:961	--
4083	3034	Archi and Biga	1982	ARET 3:962	--
4084	3035	Archi and Biga	1982	ARET 3:959	--
4085	3036	Archi and Biga	1982	ARET 3:963	Pl. XXII
4086	3037	Archi and Biga	1982	ARET 3:964	--
4087	3038	Archi and Biga	1982	ARET 3:965	--
4088	3039	Archi and Biga	1982	ARET 3:966	--
4089	3040	Archi and Biga	1982	ARET 3:967	--
4090	3041	Archi and Biga	1982	ARET 3:968	--
4091	3042	Archi and Biga	1982	ARET 3:969	--
4092	3043	Archi and Biga	1982	ARET 3:970	--
4093	3044	Archi and Biga	1982	ARET 3:971	--
4094	3045	Archi and Biga	1982	ARET 3:972	--
4095	3046	Archi and Biga	1982	ARET 3:963	Pl. XXII

TM. 75.G.	MEE 1	Editor	Date	Publication	Photo
4096	3047	Archi and Biga	1982	ARET 3:973	--
4097	3048	Archi and Biga	1982	ARET 3:974	--
4098	3049	Archi and Biga	1982	ARET 3:975	--
4099	3050	Archi and Biga	1982	ARET 3:976	--
4100	3051	Archi and Biga	1982	ARET 3:959	--
4101	3052	Archi and Biga	1982	ARET 3:951	--
4106	3057	Archi and Biga	1982	ARET 3:964	--
4107	3058	Archi and Biga	1982	ARET 3:964	--
4263	3214	Pettinato	1981d	MEE 3:29	--
4291	3242	Pettinato	1981d	MEE 3:64	--
4295	3246	Pettinato	1982a	MEE 4:58	--
4504	3455	Pettinato	1982a	MEE 4:3	--
4515	3466	Pettinato	1981d	MEE 3:4	--
4516	3467	Pettinato	1981d	MEE 3:14	--
4518	3469	Pettinato	1982a	MEE 4:67	--
4519	3470	Pettinato	1981d	MEE 3:76	--
4520	3471	Pettinato	1982a	MEE 4:30	--
4525	3476	Pettinato	1982a	MEE 4:65	--
4526	3477	Pettinato	1982a	MEE 4:2	--
4534	3485	Pettinato	1982a	MEE 4:17	--
4538	3489	Pettinato	1982a	MEE 4:62	--
4539	3490	Pettinato	1982a	MEE 4:61	--
4541	3492	Pettinato	1982a	MEE 4:68	--
4542	3493	Pettinato	1981d	MEE 3:20	--
4546	3497	Pettinato	1982a	MEE 4:94	--
4551	3502	Pettinato	1982a	MEE 4:16	--
4553	3504	Pettinato	1981d	MEE 3:27	--
4554	3505	Pettinato	1982a	MEE 4:69	--
4556	3507	Pettinato	1982a	MEE 4:95	--
4650	3601	Pettinato	1981d	MEE 3:21	--
4661	3612	Pettinato	1981d	MEE 3:28	--
5073	4024	Pettinato	1982a	MEE 4:70	--
5176	4127	Pettinato	1981d	MEE 3:30	--
5187	4138	Pettinato	1981d	MEE 3:31	--
5189	4140	Pettinato	1981d	MEE 3:32	--
5196	4147	Pettinato	1981d	MEE 3:15	--
5230	4181	Pettinato	1981d	MEE 3:33	--
5253	4204	Pettinato	1981d	MEE 3:54a	Pl. XXIX
5257	4208	Pettinato	1981d	MEE 3:8	--
5258	4209	Pettinato	1981d	MEE 3:9	--
5259	4210	Pettinato	1981d	MEE 3:5	--

TM. 75.G.	MEE 1	Editor	Date	Publication	Photo
5266	4217	Pettinato	1982a	MEE 4:66	--
5270	4221	Pettinato	1981d	MEE 3:16	--
5305	4256	Pettinato	1982a	MEE 4:27	--
5314	4265	Pettinato	1982a	MEE 4:45	--
5641	4592	Pettinato	1981d	MEE 3:49	--
5652	4603	Pettinato	1982a	MEE 4:33	--
5653	4604	Pettinato	1982a	MEE 4:36	--
5655	4606	Pettinato	1982a	MEE 4:37	--
5656	4607	Pettinato	1982a	MEE 4:44	--
5661	4612	Pettinato	1982a	MEE 4:60	--
5789	4740	Pettinato	1981d	MEE 3:58	--
5798	4749	Pettinato	1982a	MEE 4:31	--
5807	4758	Pettinato	1981d	MEE 3:41	--
5879b	4831	Pettinato	1981d	MEE 3:34	--
10007	4910	Archi	1981d	SEb 4:181-9	Fig. 44
10014	4917	Pettinato	1982a	MEE 4:19	--
10018	4921	Pettinato	1982a	MEE 4:96	--
10023	4926	Pettinato	1982a	MEE 4:63	--
10025	4928	Pettinato	1981d	MEE 3:22	--
10027	4930	Pettinato	1982a	MEE 4:20	--
10230	--	Archi	1980b	Allevam. 5f.	Pl. III 4f.
11006	4946	Pettinato	1982a	MEE 4:97	--
11010	4950	Pettinato	1979c	OA 18:177-86	--
11046	4986	Pettinato	1979c	OA 18:177-86	--
11047	4987	Pettinato	1979c	OA 18:177-86	--
11073	5013	Pettinato	1979c	OA 18:177-86	--
11079	5019	Pettinato	1979c	OA 18:177-86	--
11081	5021	Pettinato	1979c	OA 18:177-86	--
11089	5029	Pettinato	1982a	MEE 4:98	--
11144	5084	Pettinato	1982a	MEE 4:18	--
11222	5162	Pettinato	1982a	MEE 4:99	--
11244	5184	Pettinato	1982a	MEE 4:59	--
11252	5192	Pettinato	1982a	MEE 4:13	--
11254	5194	Pettinato	1982a	MEE 4:38	--
11255	5195	Pettinato	1982a	MEE 4:51	--
11258	5198	Pettinato	1981d	MEE 3:23	--
11261	5201	Pettinato	1982a	MEE 4:100	--
11262	5202	Pettinato	1982a	MEE 4:35	--
11265	5205	Pettinato	1982a	MEE 4:101	--
11267	5207	Pettinato	1982a	MEE 4:102	--
11269	5209	Pettinato	1982a	MEE 4:41	--
11270	5210	Pettinato	1982a	MEE 4:103	--
11271	5211	Pettinato	1982a	MEE 4:104	--
11274	5214	Pettinato	1982a	MEE 4:42	--
11276	5216	Pettinato	1982a	MEE 4:105	--
11277	5217	Pettinato	1982a	MEE 4:106	--
11286	5226	Pettinato	1982a	MEE 4:108	--
11288	5228	Pettinato	1982a	MEE 4:109	--
11289	5229	Pettinato	1982a	MEE 4:72	--

TM. 75.G.	MEE 1	Editor	Date	Publication	Photo
11290	5230	Pettinato	1982a	MEE 4:110	--
11291	5231	Pettinato	1981d	MEE 3:36	--
11294	5234	Pettinato	1982a	MEE 4:111	--
11295	5235	Pettinato	1982a	MEE 4:107	--
11300	5240	Pettinato	1982a	MEE 4:43	--
11301	5241	Pettinato	1982a	MEE 4:64	--
11303	5243	Pettinato	1982a	MEE 4:112	--
11304	5244	Pettinato	1982a	MEE 4:15	--
11306	5246	Pettinato	1982a	MEE 4:25	--
11307	5247	Pettinato	1982a	MEE 4:22	--
11308	5248	Pettinato	1982a	MEE 4:34	--
11311	5251	Pettinato	1982a	MEE 4:26	--
11312	5252	Pettinato	1982a	MEE 4:50	--
11317	5257	Pettinato	1982a	MEE 4:71	--
11319	5259	Pettinato	1982a	MEE 4:49	--
11323	5263	Pettinato	1982a	MEE 4:113	--
11324	5264	Pettinato	1982a	MEE 4:54	--
11327	5267	Pettinato	1982a	MEE 4:21	--
15291	5272	Pettinato	1981d	MEE 3:10	--
15299	5280	Pettinato	1982a	MEE 4:114	--
15301	5282	Pettinato	1982a	MEE 4:46	--
15309	5290	Pettinato	1981d	MEE 3:37	--
15311	5292	Pettinato	1982a	MEE 4:55	--
15312	5293	Pettinato	1981d	MEE 3:38	--
20093	5388	Pettinato	1982a	MEE 4:53	--
20102	5397	Pettinato	1982a	MEE 4:52	--
20231	5426	Pettinato	1981d	MEE 3:35	--
20277	5472	Pettinato	1981d	MEE 3:11	--
20278	5473	Pettinato	1982a	MEE 4:14	--
20279	5474	Pettinato	1981d	MEE 3:24	--
20280	5475	Pettinato	1981d	MEE 3:25	--
20306	5501	Pettinato	1981d	MEE 3:17	--
20326	5521	Pettinato	1981d	MEE 3:60	--
20580	5775	Pettinato	1982a	MEE 4:23	--
20595	5790	Pettinato	1981d	MEE 3:42	--

Ebla Texts: 1976 Season

TM. 76.G.	MEE 1	Editor	Date	Publication	Photo
35	6272	Pettinato	1981d	MEE 3:75	--
89	6301	Pettinato	1981b	Archives 94	--
412	6517	Kupper	1980	SEb 2:49-50	Fig. 13
523	6521	Pettinato	1979	OLA 5:204-33	--
523	6521	Pettinato	1981b	Archives 203-25	--

Ebla Bibliography

d'Agostino, Franco

    1982   L'inno al "Signore del Cielo e della Terra": la quarta linea della composizione. OA 21: 27-30.

Alberti, Amedeo

    1979   Sul valore della misura "mun-du." OA 18: 217-224.

    1981   TM.75.G.1353 un singulare "bilancio a pareggio" da Ebla. OA 20: 37-49.

Archi, Alfonso

    1979a   The Epigraphic Evidence from Ebla and the Old Testament. Biblica 60: 556-566.

    1979b ^{d}Ià-ra-mu at Ebla. SEb 1: 45-48 and figure 15 a-c.

    1979c   An Administrative Practice and the "Sabbatical Year" at Ebla. SEb 1: 91-95 and figures 21-24.

    1979d   Diffusione del culto di ^{D}NI-da-kul. SEb 1: 105-113 and figures 33a-35b.

    1979/80   Les Dieux d'Ebla au IIIe millenaire avant J.C. et les dieux d'Ugarit. AAAS 29/30: 167-171.

    1980a   Considerazioni sul sistema ponderale di Ebla. AdE1: 1-29 and plates I-VIII (preprint).

    1980b   Allevamento e distributione del bestiame ad Ebla. AdE1: 1-33 and plates I-XII (preprint).

    1980c   Notes on Eblaite Geography. SEb 2: 1-16 and figures 1a-5c.

    1980d   Ancora su Ebla e la Bibbia. SEb 2: 17-40 and figure 6.

    1980e   Les textes lexicaux bilingues d'Ebla. SEb 2: 81-89.

    1980f   Un testo matematico d'età protosiriana. SEb 3: 63-64 and figure 15 a-b.

1981a   Notes on Eblaite Geography II. <u>SEb</u> 4: 1-17 and plates 1-5.

1981b   Kiš nei testi di Ebla. <u>SEb</u> 4: 77-87.

1981c   I rapporti tra Ebla e Mari. <u>SEb</u> 4: 129-166 and figures 35a-431.

1981d   La "Lista di nomi e professioni" ad Ebla. <u>SEb</u> 4: 177-204 and figure 44 a-d.

1981e   A Mythologem in Eblaitology: Mesilim of Kish at Ebla. <u>SEb</u> 4: 227-230.

1981f   Further Concerning Ebla and the Bible. <u>BA</u> 44: 145-154. English translation of 1980d.

1982   Wovon lebte man in Ebla? <u>AfO</u> <u>Beiheft</u> 19: 173-188 and Figures 1-25.

Archi, Alfonso and Biga, Maria Giovanna

1982   <u>Testi Amministrativi di Vario Contenuo (Archivio L. 2769: TM.75.G.3000-4101)</u> ARET 3. Rome.

Biga, Maria Giovanna

1981   Tre testi amministrativi da Ebla. <u>SEb</u> 4: 25-33 and figures 11a-13b.

Biggs, Robert D.

1980   The Ebla Tablets: An Interim Perspective. <u>BA</u> 43: 76-87.

1981   Ebla and Abu Salabikh: The Linguistic and Literary Aspects. Pp. 121-133 in Cagni 1981.

1982   The Ebla Tablets: A 1981 Perspective. <u>BSMS</u> 2: 9-24.

Brugnatelli, Vermondo

1982   Per un'interpretazione di TM.75.G.1392. <u>OA</u> 21:31-32.

Butz, Kilian

1981   Zur Terminologie der Viehwirtschaft in den Texten aus Ebla. Pp. 321-353 in Cagni 1981

Cagni, Luigi (ed.)

1981   La lingua di Ebla. Atti del Convegno
        internazionale (Napoli, 21-23 aprile 1980).
        Naples.

Caplice, Richard I.

1981   Eblaite and Akkadian. Pp. 161-164 in Cagni
        1981.

Castellino, Giorgio R.

1981   Marginal Notes on Ebla. Pp. 235-240 in
        Cagni 1981.

Charpin, Dominique

1982   Mari et le calendrier d'Ebla. RA 76: 1-6.

Civil, Miguel

1982   Studies on Early Dynastic Lexicography. I.
        OA 21: 1-26.

Dahood, Mitchell

1978   Ebla, Ugarit and the Old Testament. VT,
        Supplement 29: 81-112.

1981a   The Linguistic Classification of Eblaite.
        Pp. 177-189 in Cagni 1981.

1981b   The Equivalents of EME-BAL in the Eblaite
        Bilinguals. OA 20: 191-194.

1981c   Eblaite i-du and Hebrew 'ēd, "Rain Cloud."
        CBQ 43: 534-538.

1982a   Hiphils and Hophals in Eblaite. OA 21:
        33-37.

1982b   Eblaite and Biblical Hebrew. CBQ 44: 1-24.

Dahood, Mitchell and Giovanni Pettinato

1977   Ugaritic ršp gn and Eblaite rasap qunu(m)^{ki}.
        OrNS 46: 230-232.

Edzard, Dietz Otto

1980   Sumerisch 1 bis 10 in Ebla. SEb 3: 121-127
        and figure 26 a-b.

1981a   Verwaltungstexte verschiedenen Inhalts (aus
        dem Archiv L.2769). ARET 2. Rome.

1981b   Der Text TM.75.G.1444 aus Ebla. SEb 4:
         35-59 and figure 14 a-i.

1981c   Neue Erwägungen zum Brief des Enna-Dagan von
         Mari (TM.75.G.2367). SEb 4: 89-97.

Fronzaroli, Pelio

1977a   West Semitic Toponymy in Northern Syria in
         the Third Millennium B.C. JSS 22: 145-166.

1977b   L'interferenza linguistica nella Siria
         settentionale del III millenio. Pp. 27-43
         in R. Ajello, ed., Interferenza linguistica.
         Atti del Convegno della Societa Italiana di
         Glottologia. Pisa.

1979a   Un atto reale di donazione dagli archivi di
         Ebla (TM.75.G.1766). SEb 1: 3-16 and
         figures 1-2.

1979b   Problemi di fonetica eblaita, 1. SEb 1:
         65-89.

1979c   The Concord in Gender in Eblaite Theophoric
         Personal Names. UF 11: 275-281.

1980a   Gli equivalenti di eme-bal nelle liste
         lessicali eblaite. SEb 2: 91-95.

1980b   Un verdetto reale dagli Archivi di Ebla
         (TM.75.G.1452). SEb 3: 33-52 and figure 9
         a-b.

1980b   Gli equivalenti di eme-bal nelle liste
         lessicali eblaite. SEb 2: 91-95.

1980c   Il verdetto per A'mur-Damu e sua madre
         (TM.75.G.1430). SEb 3: 65-78 and figure 16
         a-d.

1981a   La congiunzione eblaita ap. SEb 4: 167-176.

1981b   Note sul contatto linguistico a Ebla. VO 3:
         33-46.

1982   La contribution de la langue d'Ebla à la
         conaissance du sémitique archaïque. Pp.
         131-146 in H.-J. Nissen and J. Renger
         (eds.), Mesopotamien und seine Nachbarn.
         Politische und kulturelle
         Wechselbeziechungen im Alten Vordersasien
         vom 4. bis 1. Jahrtausend v. Chr. Berlin.
         (= XXV CRRAI)

Garbini, Giovanni

   1976   "Paleo-siriano" megūm = "lega, federazione".
               AION 36: 222-225.

   1978a   Pensieri su Ebla (ovvero: Le ouva di
               Babilonia). AION 38: 41-52.

   1978b   La lingua di Ebla. La Parola del Passato
               33: 241-259.

   1981   Considerations on the Language of Ebla. Pp.
               75-82 in Cagni 1981.

Gelb, Ignace J.

   1977   Thoughts about Ibla: A Preliminary
               Evaluation, March 1977. SMS 1: 3-30.

   1981   Ebla and the Kish Civilization. Pp. 9-73 in
               Cagni 1981.

Grégoire, Jean-Pierre

   1981   Remarques sur quelques noms de fonction et
               sur l'organisation administrative dans les
               archives d'Ebla. Pp. 379-399 in Cagni 1981.

Hass, Volkert

   1981   Zwei Gottheiten aus Ebla in hethitischer
               Überlieferung. OA 20: 251-257.

Hecker, Karl

   1981   Eigennamen und die Sprache von Ebla. Pp.
               165-175 in Cagni 1981.

Kienast, Burkhart

   1980   Der Feldzugsbericht des Ennadagan in
               literarhistorischer Sicht. OA 19: 247-261.

   1981   Die Sprache von Ebla und das Altsemitische.
               Pp. 83-98 in Cagni 1981.

Krebernik, Manfred

   1982   Zu Syllabar und Orthographie der
               lexikalischen Texte aus Ebla. Teil I. ZA
               72: 178-236.

   1983   Zu Syllabar und Orthographie der
               lexikalischen Texte aus Ebla. Teil 2

(Glossar). ZA 73: 1-47.

Krecher, Joachim

1981   Sumerogramme und syllabische Orthographie in
            den Texten aus Ebla. Pp. 135-154 in Cagni
            1981.

Lambert, Wilfred G.

1981a   The Language of Ebla and Akkadian. Pp.
            155-160 in Cagni 1981.

1981b   The statue inscription of Ibbiṭ-Lim of Ebla.
            RA 75: 95-96.

Lipiński, Edward

1981   Formes verbales dans les nomes propres
            d'Ebla et système verbal sémitique. Pp.
            191-210 in Cagni 1981.

de Maigret, Alessandro

1980   Riconsiderazioni sul sistema ponderale di
            Ebla. OA 19: 161-169.

1981   Il fattore idrologico nell'economia di Ebla.
            OA 20: 1-36 and plates I-II.

Mander, Pietro

1979   Presenza di scongiure én-é-nu-ru ad Ebla.
            OrNS 48: 335-339.

1980   Coeva documentazione mesopotamica per il sa-
            za^{ki} "governatorato" di Ebla. OA 19:
            263-264.

1982   Osservazioni al testo amministrativo di Ebla
            MEE I 1453 (= ARET II 13). OA 21: 227-236.

Matthiae, Paolo

1975   Ebla nel periodo delle dinastie amorree e
            della dinastia di Akkad. Scoperte
            archeologiche recenti a Tell Mardikh. OrNS
            44: 337-360 and plates XXIX-XXXVIII.
            English translation: Ebla in the period of
            the Amorite Dynasties and the Dynasty of
            Akkad: Recent Archeological Discoveries at
            Tell Mardikh. MANE 1/6 (1979).

1975/76   La biblioteca reale di Ebla (2400-2250

65

B.C.). Risultati della Missione Archeologica Italiana in Siria, 1975. RendPARA 48: 19-45.

1976b Ebla à l'époque d'Akkad: archéologie et histoire. CRAI: 190-215.

1976c Ebla in the Late Early Syrian Period: the Royal Palace and the State Archives. BA 39: 94-113.

1976d Aspetti amministrativi e topografici di Ebla nel III millennio av. Cr. B. Considerazioni archeologiche. RSO 50: 16-30.

1977a Le palais royal protosyrien d'Ebla: nouvelles recherches archéologiques à Tell Mardikh en 1976. CRAI: 148-174.

1977b Le Palais Royal et les Archives d'Etat d'Ebla protosyrienne. Akkadica 2: 2-19.

1977c Ebla, un imperio ritrovato. Turin.

1979 DU-UB^{ki} di Mardikh IIB1 = TU-BA^{ki} di Alalakh VII. SEb 1: 115-118.

1981 Ebla: An Empire Rediscovered. Garden City. [English translation of 1977c].

1982 The Problem of the Relations Between Ebla and Mesopotamia in the Time of the Royal Palace of Mardikh IIB1. Pp. 125-130 in H.-J. Nissen and J. Renger (eds.), Mesopotamien und seine Nachbarn. Politische und kulturelle Wechselbeziehungen im Alten Vorderasien vom 4. bis 1. Jahrtausend v. Chr (= XXV CRRAI). Berlin.

Matthiae, P. and G. Pettinato

1967/68 Il torso di Ibbit-Lim, re di Ebla. MAIS: 1-38 (preprint).

Michalowski, Piotr

1984a Review of Edzard 1981a. Forthcoming in JNES.

1984b Third Millennium Contacts. Observations on the Relationships between Mari and Ebla. Forthcoming in Gordon D. Young, ed., Mari at 50: Studies in Honor of the 50th Anniversary of the Discovery of Tell Hariri-Mari Winona

Lake.

Milano, Lucio

1980   Due rendiconti metalli da Ebla. SEb 3: 1-21
            and figures 1a-2m.

Morrison, M. A.

1983   A New Anchor Axehead. OA. In press.

Müller, Hans-Peter

1980   Die Texte aus Ebla. Eine Herausforderung an
            die alttestamentliche Wissenschaft. BZ 24:
            161-179.

1981a   Gab es in Ebla einen Gottesnamen Ja? ZA 70:
            70-92.

1981b   Das eblaitische Verbalsystem nach den bicher
            veröffentlichten Personennamen. Pp. 211-233
            in Cagni 1981.

Nissen, Hans J.

1981   Bemerkungen zur Listenliteratur Vorderasiens
            im 3. Jahrtausend (gesehen von den
            archaischen Texten von Uruk). Pp. 99-108 in
            Cagni 1981.

Pennacchietti, Fabrizio A.

1981   Indicazioni preliminari sul sistema
            preposizionale dell'eblaita. Pp. 291-319 in
            Cagni 1981.

Petráček, Karel

1979   Die semitische Laryngaltheorie und die
            Sprache von Ibla. AION 39: 385-394.

Pettinato, Giovanni

1970   Inscription de Ibbit-Lim, roi de Ebla. AAA
            20: 73-76.

1974/77   Il calendario di Ebla al tempo del re Ibbi-
            Sipiš sulla base di TM.75.G.427. AfO 25:
            1-36.

1975   Testi cuneiformi del 3. millennio in paleo-
            cananeo rinvenuti nella campagna 1974 a
            Tell-Mardĩkh = Ebla. OrNS 44: 361-374.

English translation: Old Canaanite Cuneiform Texts of the Third Millennium. MANE 1/7 (1979).

1975/6   I testi cuneiformi della Biblioteca Reale di Tell Mardikh-Ebla. RendPARA 48: 47-57.

1976a   ED LU E ad Ebla. La ricostruzione delle prime 63 righe sulla base di TM.75.G.1488. OA 15:169-178 and plate III.

1976b   The Royal Archives of Tell Mardikh-Ebla. BA 39: 44-52.

1976c   Carchemiš - Kār-Kamiš. Le prime attestazioni del III millennio. OA 15: 11-15.

1976d   Aspetti amministrativi e topografici di Ebla nel III millennio av. Cr. A. Documentazione epigrafica. RSO 50: 1-15.

1976e   Ibla (Ebla). A. Philologisch. RlA 5: 9-13.

1977a   Relations entre les royaumes d'Ebla et de Mari au troisieme millenaire d'apres les Archives Royales de Tell Mardikh-Ebla. Akkadica 2: 20-28.

1977b   Gli Archivi Reali di Tell Mardikh-Ebla: Riflessioni e prospettive. RBI 25: 225-243.

1977c   Il calendario semitico del 3. millennio riconstruito sulla base dei testi di Ebla. OA 16: 257-285 and plates XI-XII.

1978a   L'Atlante Geografico nel Vicino Oriente Antico attestato ad Ebla ed ad Abū Ṣalābīkh (I). OrNS 47: 50-73 and plates VII-XII.

1978b   Liste presargoniche di uccelli nella documentazione di Fara ed Ebla. OA 17: 165-178 and plates XIV-XVI.

1979a   Le collezioni én-é-nu-ru di Ebla. OA 18: 329-351 and plates XXXVI-XLII.

1979b   Catalogo dei Testi Cuneiformi di Tell Mardikh-Ebla. MEE 1. Naples.

1979c   Culto ufficiale ad Ebla durante il regno di Ibbi-Sippiš. Con Appendice di Pietro Mander. OA 18: 85-215 and plates I-XII. Also

68

published separately as OA Collectio vol. XVI. Rome 1979.

1979d   Die Lesung von AN.IM.DUGUD.MUŠEN nach einem Ebla-Text. JCS 31: 116-117.

1979e   Ebla, un impero inciso nell'argilla. Milan.

1979f   Il commercio internazionale di Ebla: Economia statale e privata. Pp. 171-233 in Edward Lipiński, ed., State and Temple Economy in the Ancient Near East I (=OLA 5). Leuven.

1980a   Testi Amministrativi della Bibliotheca L. 2769. MEE 2. Naples.

1980b   Ebla e la Bibba. OA 19: 49-72 and plates III-IV.

1980c   Bolletino militare della campagna di Ebla contro la città di Mari. OA 19: 231-245 and plates XIV-XV.

1980d   Pre-Ugaritic Documentation of Ba'al. Pp. 203-209 in G. Rendsburg et al. (eds.), The Bible World. Essays in Honor of Cyrus H. Gordon. New York: KATV.

1980e   Ebla and the Bible. BA 43: 203-216.

1981a   I vocabolari bilingui di Ebla. Problemi di traduzione e di lessicografia sumerico-eblaita. Pp. 241-276 and plates I-II in Cagni 1981.

1981b   The Archives of Ebla: An Empire Inscribed in Clay. Garden City. [English translation of 1979e].

1981c   Gasur nella Documentazione Epigrafica Di Ebla. Pp. 297-304 in M. A. Morrison and D. I. Owen, eds., Studies on the Civilization and Culture of Nuzi and the Hurrians. Winona Lake.

1981d   Testi Lessicali Monolingui della Bibliotheca L. 2769. MEE 3. Naples.

1981e   La pronuncia sumerica dei numeri da 1 a 10 in un testo lessicale di Ebla. AION 41: 141-143 and Plate 1.

1982a   Testi Lessicali Bilingui della Biblioteca

L. 2769. MEE 4. Naples.

1982b Die königlichen Archive von Tell Mardikh-Ebla aus dem 3. Jahrtausend v. Chr. Pp. 251-261 in Palast und Hütte. Beiträge zum Bauen und Wohnen im Altertum. Tagungsbeiträge eines Symposiums der Alexander von Humboldt-Stiftung Bonn-Bad Godesbeurg veranstaltet vom 25.-30. November 1979 in Berlin. Mainz am Rhein.

Picchioni, Sergio A.

1980 La direzione della scrittura cuneiforme e gli archivi di Tell Mardikh-Ebla. OrNS 49: 225-251.

1981a Osservazioni sulla paleografia e sulla cronologia dei testi di Ebla. Pp. 109-120 in Cagni 1981.

1981b Riconstruzione segmentale del testo storico TM.75.G.2420. OA 20: 187-190.

Pomponio, Francesco

1980a AO 7754 ed il sistema ponderale di Ebla. OA 19: 171-186.

1980b Review of Pettinato 1979b and 1979e. RSO 54: 227-237.

1983 Mešeq di Gen. 15,2 e un termine amministrativo di Ebla. Bibbia e Oriente 25 (no. 136): 107-110.

Saporetti, Claudio

1981 Una considerazione sul testo n. 6527 del Catalogo di Ebla. Pp. 287-289 in Cagni 1981.

Scandone-Matthiae, G.

1979/80 Ebla et l'Egypte a l'ancien et au moyen empire. AAAS 29/30: 189-199.

1982 Inscriptions royales égyptiennes de l'ancien empire a Ebla. Pp. 125-130 in H.-J. Nissen and J. Renger (eds.), Mesopotamien und seine Nachbarn. Politische und kulturelle Wechselbeziehungen im Alten Vordersasien vom 4. bis 1. Jahrtausend v. Chr. (= XXV CRRAI). Berlin.

von Soden, Wolfram

1981   Das Nordsemitische in Babylonien und in
               Syrien. Pp. 355-361 in Cagni 1981.

Sollberger, Edmond

1980   The So-Called Treaty Between Ebla and
               "Ashur." SEb 3: 130-155 and plate 27.

Steinkeller, Piotr

1983   · The Eblaite Preposition gidimay "Before."
               OA. In press.

Ullendorf, Edward

1978   Review of Gelb 1977. JSS 23: 151-154.

Vattioni, Francesco

1981   Apporto del semitico di nord-ovest per la
               compresione della lessicografia eblaita.
               Pp. 277-285 in Cagni 1981.

Waetzoldt, Hartmut

1981   Zur Terminologie der Metalle in den Texten
               aus Ebla. Pp. 363-378 in Cagni 1981.